WINE & DINE AT HOME

WINE & DINE AT HOME

Easy recipes & perfect pairings

Charlotte Kristensen

MITCHELL BEAZLEY

For the friends who carried me through xx

First published in Great Britain in 2026 by
Mitchell Beazley, an imprint of
Octopus Publishing Group Ltd
Carmelite House
50 Victoria Embankment
London EC4Y 0DZ
www.octopusbooks.co.uk

An Hachette UK Company
www.hachette.co.uk

ISBN 978-1-84601-642-4
eISBN 798-1-84601-643-1

A CIP catalogue record for this book is available from the British Library.

Printed and bound in China

10 9 8 7 6 5 4 3 2 1

FSC www.fsc.org MIX Paper | Supporting responsible forestry FSC® C008047

Publishing Director Alison Starling
Art Director Juliette Norsworthy
Senior Editor Alex Stetter
Photographer Laura Jalbert
Food Stylist Natalie Thomson
Prop Stylist Max Robinson
Recipe Consultant Elizabeth Pearson
Wine Shoot Producer Janina Doyle
Illustrator Kailee Keefe-Skaberna (Kiki Makes)
Assistant Production Manager Lisa Pinnell

CONTENTS

INTRODUCTION

I fell for wine the way many of us do: with bottles opened and shared at the table, alongside delicious food and great company. For me, food, wine and lively conversation are just meant to be together – with the wine pairing elevating a meal into a memorable moment.

Whenever I'm thinking about a menu, whether I'm cooking at home or dining out, I'm always thinking about the wine choice – what would match this plate, what would lift that dish, what would be a clever pairing or just utterly irresistible together? Over the years, I've taken so much pleasure in talking about, writing about, planning and creating wine and food pairings – classic or contemporary, those that capture a place or a personal memory. Pairings that warm the heart, stir emotion, or are simply mouth-watering.

This book focuses on easy at-home recipes to make wine pairing accessible – something that can be enjoyed by everyone, not just connoisseurs, from everyday occasions to special events. The pairings are meant to be fun and inviting, designed to encourage and inspire you to discover new grape varieties and styles, or to revisit some of your favourite wines with a new perspective. To embrace the sensory pleasure of matching food and wine.

This book is divided into three parts:

- **Part 1: DISCOVER** introduces some of the key concepts of food and wine pairing, recognizing that it combines principles (the science), play (an artistic element) and experience (our library of sensory encounters).
- **Part 2: PAIR** shares 50 easy-to-recreate at-home pairings in the following categories: apéro, boards and nibbles; fish and seafood; poultry and meat; vegetarian and cheese; and sweet.
- **Part 3: CURATE** offers themed menus, experiences and ideas for wine get-togethers.

So, get comfy, pour yourself a glass, grab a little something to nibble on – and let's dive into the wonderful world of food and wine pairing.

PART 1

DISCOVER

INTRODUCTION TO WINE AND FOOD PAIRING

I approach wine and food pairing as something that's meant to be enriching – of course, there are some key principles that provide a framework to our understanding, but fundamentally, pairing is an exercise in pleasure and getting to know what your palate likes. This part of the book recognizes the various elements that play a role in the art and enjoyment of food and wine pairing.

To begin with, we look at the science part, the **Principles** of food and wine pairing, focusing on the common interactions people sense when pairing certain types of food with wine, looking specifically at salt, acidity, fat, sweetness, spice, bitterness and umami. Each of these sections opens with a visual to stimulate your mind and appetite around one of these essential elements – drawing out those foods and wines that epitomize each of these concepts.

We then turn to some of the more artistic and fluid aspects of food and wine pairing, which are grouped under **Play**. Here is where we explore the more creative concepts of flavour intensity, flavour synergy, touch and terroir matching.

This part concludes with **Experience**, which recognizes that our sensory experience of food and wine matching is unique to our DNA and life encounters. The chapter ends with white and red wine wheels, which broadly arrange common grape varieties from lightest to boldest in style, grouped by shared characteristics, followed by quick guides to pairing food with ten of the most common white and red grape varieties, and an introduction to pairing food with sparkling, rosé, orange and fortified wines.

BROLIO
2023
RICASOLI
LUSTAU
Fino
DEL PUERTO
JEREZ-XÉRÈS-SHERRY
ÉPERNAY - FRANCE

WINE & SALT

WINE & SALT

Salt is wine's best friend: it enhances fruity notes and a wine's texture while softening acidity and tannins. I regularly jest that if you have a boring, light, flavourless and high-acid white wine, just serve it alongside some salty snacks for an instant upgrade. And an entry-level red wine with astringent tannins, which feels almost impossible to drink on its own, will soften when paired with a robust salty dish. Let's look into this further.

HOW SALT INTERACTS WITH WINE

- **A wine can feel less acidic and its tannins less astringent** The addition of salt reduces our perception of acidity and makes tannins feel less drying, grippy and astringent, similar to how salt softens the astringency of meat or rounds out sourness in cooking.
- **A wine can feel fruitier, with a rounder body** As acidity and tannins soften, the fruit character becomes more dominant and the body may seem smoother, rounder and fuller.

WINES TO PAIR WITH SALTY FOOD

- **High-acid white wines** Unoaked Chardonnay (such as Chablis), Muscadet and Albariño are great matches with naturally salty shellfish and salty snacks.
- **Dry Sherry** The tangy nature of dry Sherry wines, such as Fino and Manzanilla, echoes the salty quality of jamón ibérico and anchovies, and the briny quality of olives.
- **High-tannin reds** Cabernet Sauvignon, Nebbiolo and similar high-tannin reds work well with salted meats or hard salty cheese.
- **Sparkling wines** Champagne and similar traditional-method sparkling wines (see page 62) pair well with salty foods, from everyday salted crisps to luxurious caviar.
- **Sweet wines** These provide a satisfying contrast with salty food – the classic match is alongside cheese.

SALTY RECIPES

Here is a selection of the recipes in this book that demonstrate the successful pairing of salty dishes with wine:

- Champagne with fish goujons, devilled eggs and caviar (see page 73)
- Chablis with scallops and samphire (see page 90)
- Picpoul de Pinet with grilled garlic mussels (see page 97)
- Sangiovese with duck ragu and pappardelle (see page 135)
- Soave with pesto pasta (see page 53)

WINES WITH A SALTY OR SALINE EDGE

While it's generally acknowledged that vines don't absorb salt at levels detectable in grapes, many grapes are recognized for producing wines that feel like they have a distinctive salty or saline edge. This characteristic is often linked to a particular grape variety, the vine's terroir (proximity to the sea, volcanic or limestone soils) and winemaking techniques, such as lees ageing and reduction. It's more about the impression of something saline and savoury than actual salt in the wine. These wines are favourites of mine for their salty mouth-watering quality and are fantastic with food.

- **Sea-breeze fresh whites** These white wines (among others) capture that sea-like salinity: Albariño from Rías Baixas, and over the border, Vinho Verde from Portugal (which often includes Alvarinho, the Portuguese spelling), Muscadet wines from the coastal region of the Loire, and the energizing wines from Picpoul de Pinet in the South of France.
- **Shell-like and reductive Chardonnay** Chardonnay from Chablis typically gives a crushed-shell-like quality, felt to be attributed to the unique limestone soils rich with fossils in the region. Further south, some Chardonnays from the Côte de Beaune are made in what is known as a reductive style (with little exposure to oxygen), which can result in a smoky, flinty quality with a saline nuance.
- **Volcanic mineral wines** Wines grown on volcanic soils are recognized for displaying a saline mineral edge, such as Assyrtiko from Santorini, the wines of Sicily (Etna Bianco/Rosso, Frappato, Nerello Mascalese) and the interesting wines of Tenerife (Listán Negro and Listán Blanco).
- **Sherry wines** The dry styles of Sherry wines, Fino and Manzanilla, can display a distinct salty and tangy quality.

THALASS
SANTORIN
E TRACY
FUME

WINE & ACIDITY

WINE & ACIDITY

Acidity injects life into both a dish and a wine – it's crucial for balance and energy. Acidity in food often has a positive effect on many styles of wine, creating harmony by adding a fresh, lifted quality to the palate. We'll explore this further here, along with the important role acidity plays in wine when pairing with certain dishes.

HOW ACIDITY IN FOOD INTERACTS WITH WINE

- **A wine can feel less acidic** Food with high acidity reduces our perception of a wine's acidity, so it tastes less sharp.
- **A wine can feel fruitier, with a rounder body** As the wine's acidity is softened, the fruit character becomes more dominant and the body may seem smoother, rounder and fuller.

WINES TO PAIR WITH HIGH-ACID DISHES

High-acid dishes generally pair best with high-acid wines. For example:

- **High-acid white wines** Dishes with lots of lemon or a vinaigrette pair well with high-acid fresh wines made from grapes such as Sauvignon Blanc, Riesling and Albariño.
- **High-acid red wines** Tomato-based dishes with lots of natural acidity pair best with reds that have high acidity, such as those made from the Italian red grapes Sangiovese, Frappato or Barbera.
- **Sparkling wines** Traditional-method sparkling wines have high acidity and stand up well to acidic ingredients (such as lemon or capers), dressings and vinaigrettes.

WINES TO GENERALLY AVOID WITH HIGH-ACID DISHES

Avoid pairing low-acid wines with high-acid dishes. For example, white wines such as Viognier that can display low acidity will feel flat with a crisp salad dressed with a sharp citrus vinaigrette (but note that there is also an imbalance between the light texture of a crisp salad and the full body of Viognier in this example).

WINES WITH HIGH ACIDITY

Here is a selection of grapes and styles that have high acidity:

- **White grapes** Riesling, Sauvignon Blanc and cool-climate Chardonnay (such as Chablis).
- **Red grapes** Pinot Noir, Cabernet Sauvignon, Frappato and Nebbiolo.
- **Other styles** Traditional-method sparkling wines, including Champagne, Cava and English sparkling wines, and sweet wines such as Tokaji and Sauternes.

As with acidic dishes, picking a wine with high acidity can be key to successful pairings with fatty, umami and sweet dishes by providing balance with these characteristics:

- **Fat** High acidity brings freshness and lift to fatty dishes.
- **Sweetness** High acidity prevents a cloying feeling from sweet dishes.
- **Umami** High acidity brightens the broad savoury nuance in umami dishes.

HIGH-ACID RECIPES

Here is a selection of the recipes in this book with high-acid elements that work well with high-acid wines.

- Dry Riesling with sea bass crudo (see page 101)
- Vinho Verde with fish tacos (see page 106)
- Frappato with tomato tart (see page 162)
- Pinot Noir with confit duck, blood orange and sweet potato (see page 131)

LANGHAM
PUDDLE
VINEYARD
CHARDONNAY
Tasmania

WINE & FAT

WINE & FAT

For me, there are few things more satisfying than a triple-cooked chip dipped in mayonnaise paired with a crisp white wine; or a perfectly charred, medium-rare, marbled rib-eye steak with a firm red. Fatty foods are a dream with the right wine, and that nirvana moment is achieved where indulgence meets lift, and everything falls into place.

HOW FAT INTERACTS WITH WINE

- **A wine can feel less astringent, with a rounder body** Fat and protein in food bind to tannins in red wine, making tannins feel less drying, grippy and astringent and giving the body a smoother, rounder, fuller feel.
- **A wine can create balance when it has good acidity** Wines with fresh acidity cut through fat, preventing a dish from tasting cloying or flat.

WINES TO PAIR WITH FATTY FOODS

- **High-acid, light-bodied wines** Fried dishes work well with crisp whites – think Albariño with croquettes, cool-climate unoaked Chardonnay with battered fish and chips. Reds with high acidity, such as Gamay (Beaujolais) or Frappato, are great matches for fatty cured meats and cheese. Fatty duck dishes and other game birds are a classic pairing with the high-acid red grape Pinot Noir. Cooler-climate rosés, such as those from the Loire or England, balance fatty or creamy dishes.
- **Textured, high-acid white wines** Wines such as white Burgundy (and similar styles of oaked Chardonnay, such as those from Oregon), Godello, Assyrtiko and Soave Classico are both textured and have present acidity, so pair well with fatty fish dishes, poultry with cream and other creamy dishes and cheese, giving lift and echoing texture.

- **High-tannin red wines** Rich, fatty meats, such as lamb, beef and pork, are best paired with high-tannin reds, such as Cabernet Sauvignon, Nebbiolo and Syrah. These all have high acidity too, further enhancing the balance of the pairing.
- **Sparkling wines** Traditional-method sparkling wines with naturally high acidity are an excellent option with fried and creamy dishes. Consider the intensity and depth of flavour in the sparkling wine to match with the dish.
- **Sweet wines** Those with high acidity, such as Sauternes, Tokaji and sweet Rieslings, balance both creamy desserts and mixed cheese boards.

WINES TO GENERALLY AVOID WITH FATTY FOODS

Avoid pairing full-bodied, low-acid wines, such as very ripe oaked Chardonnay, Viognier or jammy high-alcohol reds, with fatty dishes as they will feel dull and cloying.

FAT-FORWARD RECIPES

Here is a selection of fatty and creamy recipes with wines that complement them well, giving balance and lift to these dishes.

- Cava with truffled cheese toasties (see page 74)
- Beaujolais with cheese and meat board (see page 88)
- Chenin Blanc with chicken, tarragon and pears (see page 128)
- Tokaji with apricot tarte Tatin (see page 176)

NOE
VORS
VERY OLD RARE SHERRY
30
2020

WINE & SWEETNESS

WINE & SWEETNESS

Let me just start by saying we've all been there: it's the end of a meal, time for dessert. Maybe you're having a slice of lemon tart, a rich chocolate pot, or sticky toffee pudding. You haven't thought about a new wine – there's still some white or red left in your glass. You take a bite of dessert, then a sip of wine – and suddenly, you're hit by that bitter, unpleasant clash between your delicious dessert and your previously lovely, dry wine. You decide to finish the dessert and come back to the wine afterwards – a wise decision. But why does this happen?

HOW SWEETNESS IN FOOD INTERACTS WITH WINE

- **A wine can feel drier and its fruit or sweetness masked** Sweet food next to a dry wine decreases the perception of fruit or sweetness, making the wine seem drier, more austere and muted.
- **A wine can taste more acidic and bitter, and its tannins more astringent** Sweetness increases the perception of acidity, making the wine seem more sour. Wines with high tannins or noticeable oak influence can feel even more drying, grippy and astringent when paired with sweet food.
- **A wine can feel more alcoholic** With fruit and sweetness dulled and bitterness accentuated, the warming effect of alcohol becomes more apparent.

WINES TO PAIR WITH SWEET FOOD

The general rule of thumb is that a wine should be at least as sweet as the dish. This is a helpful starting point that will generally steer you clear of pairing dry wines with sweet food and lead you to stick to wines that are at a minimum off-dry. (But note, although this is the rule, we all have our personal preferences, and I personally enjoy a few exceptions to the rule. See Experience on pages 44–5 for more.)

SWEET FOOD AND SWEET WINE PAIRINGS

Here are some classic pairings of sweet foods with a range of sweet wine styles from key regions:

- ✦ Dark (bittersweet) chocolate with Port from Portugal (fortified)
- ✦ Crème brûlée and other creamy and caramelized desserts with Sauternes from France
- ✦ Apple tart, rich citrus, honey and spice with Tokaji from Hungary
- ✦ Lemon or citrus-based tarts or desserts with sweet Riesling from Germany
- ✦ Treacle tart or nutty, rich, molasses-based desserts with Madeira from Portugal (fortified)
- ✦ Tarte Tatin and similar honeyed orchard fruit, pastries or crumbles with late-harvest or sweet Chenin from the Loire, France
- ✦ Light and fruity desserts, such as pavlova, with Moscato d'Asti from Italy

For more on pairing food with sweet wines, see pages 64–5.

OTHER DISHES TO PAIR WITH SWEET WINES

Sweet and salty, and sweet and spicy, are two contrasting combinations that are intriguing and satisfying on the palate. Classic combinations include:

- ✦ Blue cheese (especially) or other cheeses with Sauternes, Tokaji (white) and Port (red/ruby or tawny).
- ✦ Spicy food with off-dry to sweeter styles of Riesling (see more on page 30).

YALUMBA
EDEN VALLEY
VIOGNIER
2022
Produce of France
2022
FLEURIE
APPELLATION D'ORIGINE PROTEGÉE
Mis en bouteille par
750 ML
13,5% VOL
GUY BRETON À 69910 VILLIÉ-MORGON

WINE & SPICE

WINE & SPICE

I'm a spice fanatic. Fresh chillies, pepper of all shades, smoky harissa paste, hot sauces of every scorch level – I love them all. I crave that depth of flavour and the gently warming to fiery heat you get from spice. But dishes with heat can pose a challenge when it comes to wine pairing, thanks to how spice interacts with alcohol, bitterness and fruit – so let's take a closer look at the best picks.

HOW SPICE INTERACTS WITH WINE

- **A wine can feel less fruity or sweet** Spice can mute or dull the perception of a wine's fruit and sweetness, making it feel more austere as alcohol and bitterness become more prominent.
- **A wine can feel more astringent** Wines with high tannins or noticeable oak influence can seem even more drying, grippy and astringent when paired with spicy food.
- **A wine can feel more alcoholic** Spice heightens the perception of alcohol, so the warming effect can dominate and even create an unpleasant burning sensation on the palate.

WINES TO PAIR WITH SPICE

- **Lower-alcohol wines** Pick lower-alcohol wines (under 13% ABV) to avoid that elevated alcoholic presence on the palate. For example, dry to sweet Riesling, Vinho Verde, Pinot Noir, Gamay (Beaujolais), light Cinsault or Frappato, and sparkling wines.
- **Fruity styles of wine and low-tannin red wines** Fresh and fruity styles of wine will feel less harsh than mineral-driven or savoury styles when paired with spice. For example, dry but fruit-forward styles of rosé (such as Languedoc, French Tavel or Spanish Garnacha Rosado), the low-alcohol wines listed above, plus fruity styles of Grenache/Garnacha and Zinfandel/Primitivo. But note that alcohol levels can be high on these grapes.
- **Sweet wines** Sweet styles of wine provide a satisfying contrasting balance with spice. It's a popular flavour combination that gives both the bite and the balm. For example, off-dry to sweeter styles of Riesling, Chenin Blanc, Pinot Gris and Gewürztraminer, or sweeter styles of sparkling wine (from the higher-dosage end of Brut to Extra-Dry or Demi-Sec).

WINES TO GENERALLY AVOID WITH SPICE

- Red wines with high alcohol (over 13% ABV), firm tannins, noticeable oak and those with a savoury profile, such as aged red Bordeaux and Rioja (Reserva and Gran Reserva labels).
- White wines with noticeable oak and high alcohol, such as oaked Californian Chardonnay or oaked white Rioja, plus very dry, lean and mineral styles of white wine, such as Chablis.

THE OVERALL FLAVOUR INTENSITY OF THE DISH

Lighter spicy dishes, such as Thai salads, mild yellow curries or pasta with fresh chilli, suit fruity wines and work well with fresh whites or light reds. Richer, meat-based dishes, such as lamb massaman or rogan josh can handle bolder, spiced reds, such as Syrah, Grenache/Garnacha, Zinfandel/Primitivo, Xinomavro and more youthful styles of red Rioja. Once you enter the ultra-spicy zone (vindaloo and the like), avoid wine altogether, as these dishes will be too overpowering – stick to beer or a fruity cocktail.

WINES WITH SPICY AROMATICS

It can be a real pleasure to echo the spice notes in wine with similar flavours in a dish. Consider Rhône Syrah, which often shows black pepper spice, or Grenache, which gives softer white pepper and warm baking spices such as clove and cinnamon. Among whites, Viognier can have hints of nutmeg and clove, Gewürztraminer brings ginger and exotic spice, and Grüner Veltliner is known for its subtle white pepper lift.

SPICE RECIPES

- Gavi with orzo, courgette, almond, lemon and chilli (see page 169)
- Off-dry Riesling with one-pot green curry (see page 124)
- Off-dry Riesling with spicy prawn noodle salad (see page 102)
- Provence rosé with spicy salmon skewers (see page 114)
- Xinomavro with harissa lamb cutlets and pistachio (see page 148)

Nikolaihof
2022
AUS DEN GÄRTEN
Grüner Veltliner
40th VINTAGE

WINE & BITTERNESS

WINE & BITTERNESS

It's fascinating how differently people respond to bitterness – in fact, it's one of the most polarizing elements in both food and wine. Tolerance is shaped partly by your DNA and partly by what you've grown up with. Some people love bitter foods – black coffee, strong tea, rocket, radicchio, chicory (endive) and dark chocolate – while for others, they're the ultimate enemy of the palate. The same goes for wine: dry or tannic styles delight some drinkers, while others find them far too bitter and drying. Let's look into bitterness and how to pair wines with those trickier ingredients.

HOW BITTER FOODS INTERACT WITH WINE

- **A wine can feel more bitter and more astringent** Bitterness in food increases our perception of bitterness and tannins in a wine, making it taste more drying and grippy.

WINES TO PAIR WITH BITTER FOODS

- **Fresh and fruity dry whites** White wines, such as New Zealand Sauvignon Blanc and Grüner Veltliner, bring fruity and zesty notes with a herbaceous nuance, which work well when paired with bitter greens, such as rocket or radicchio.
- **Low-tannin red wines** Grapes such as Pinot Noir, Gamay, Grenache/Garnacha, Frappato and Cinsault have lower levels of tannin, so can work well with charred dishes.
- **Sweet wines** Sweetness can balance bitterness but be mindful of balancing intensity. For example, pair an off-dry Riesling with bitter greens, Port with bitter dark (bittersweet) chocolate, coffee-based desserts with Pedro Ximenez Sherry.

WINES TO GENERALLY AVOID WITH BITTER FOODS

As with spice, it's best to avoid red wines with firm tannins, such as young Cabernet Sauvignon or wines made from Nebbiolo, such as Barolo, and wines with noticeable oak, such as heavily oaked Chardonnay, when serving bitter foods.

RECIPES WITH BITTER INGREDIENTS

Here is a selection of recipes with some bitter elements that work well with their selected wines.

- ✦ Sauvignon Blanc with a veggie platter and whipped feta dip (see page 78)
- ✦ Grüner Veltliner with a herby trout salad (see page 110)
- ✦ Pinot Noir with confit duck, blood orange and sweet potato (see page 131)

GRAVNER

Gramona
Imperial
Domaine
VIN JAUNE
ARBOIS
APPELLATION ARBOIS CONTRÔLÉE

WINE & UMAMI

WINE & UMAMI

Umami is that gorgeously enveloping savouriness you find in ingredients such as mushrooms, truffle, eggs, shellfish, cheese, meat, soy and miso. It brings earthiness, meatiness and depth to a dish, and in cooking it's often balanced by salt or acidity to give it lift. Umami-rich dishes can be tricky to pair with wine, but the right bottle – especially one that echoes that inviting umami earthiness – can bring magic.

HOW UMAMI INTERACTS WITH WINE

- **A wine can feel less fruity or sweet** Like spice, umami can dull the perception of a wine's fruitiness or sweetness, making it feel more austere.
- **A wine can feel more acidic and its tannins more astringent** With fruit muted, acidity stands out, and wines with high tannins or noticeable oak can taste even more drying and grippy.

WINES TO PAIR WITH UMAMI

- **White and red wines with depth of fruit** Fruit-forward styles of Pinot Noir (New Zealand), fruity styles of Grenache/ Garnacha, and fruity and fresh white wines such as Albariño and New Zealand Sauvignon Blanc balance the savouriness of umami-rich dishes.
- **High-acid wines** Wines across the colour spectrum pair well with umami-rich food, cutting through and providing lift. Think traditional-method sparkling wines, such as Cava and Champagne, high-acid whites such as Chardonnay and Riesling, and reds such as Pinot Noir and Gamay (Beaujolais).
- **Wines with bottle age or umami nuances** Synergy between umami in a dish and umami-driven notes in wine can be a very enticing combination (see wine examples opposite). However, be mindful that some umami-rich wines, such as aged reds (Nebbiolo or Cabernet Sauvignon, for example), can still have firm tannins. These pairings can be challenging – the combination of savoury flavours and residual tannin may accentuate bitterness or dryness. I find that creamy textures in food can help soften tannic grip, while the wine's acidity offers a balancing lift.

WINES TO GENERALLY AVOID WITH UMAMI

It's best to avoid red wines with firm tannins and wines with noticeable oak (as we saw with spice on page 31). Very dry, lean or mineral-driven white wines – such as certain styles of Chablis (particularly Petit Chablis) – can feel austere when paired with umami-rich food. But shellfish (particularly crab, lobster, scallops and prawns/shrimp) tends to be an exception, thanks to its natural sweetness and saltiness, which help balance and soften the umami.

WINES WITH AN UMAMI CHARACTER

Here are some examples of wines that can display a distinct umami character.

- **Chardonnay, aged Champagne and Vin Jaune** These often show nutty, earthy qualities with age.
- **Sherry wines** Some styles have briny and nutty notes.
- **Pinot Noir and Nebbiolo** These wines can develop mushroom, truffle and earthy notes with age.
- **Aged Bordeaux and Rioja** These can take on more leather and meaty characteristics.

RECIPES WITH UMAMI

Here is a selection of umami-driven recipes that work well with their wines.

- Cava with truffled cheese toasties (see page 74)
- Chablis with scallops and samphire (see page 90)
- Albariño with clams in white wine (see page 93)
- Sauvignon Blanc with pea and asparagus frittata (see page 154)
- Nebbiolo with mushroom and truffle tagliatelle (see page 157)
- Champagne with mac and cheese (see page 165)

FLAVOUR INTENSITY

When it comes to the flavour intensity of a wine and a dish, consider the depth and weight of flavour in the dish, and whether you would like the wine to match or contrast with that intensity.

MATCHING FLAVOUR INTENSITY

For harmony across the dish and the glass, consider pairing depth and weight of flavour, such as:

- Rich red wines (Cabernet Sauvignon, Syrah, Malbec) with deeply flavoured slow-cooked stews.
- Medium-bodied whites (dry quality Chenin Blanc or oaked Chardonnay from Burgundy) or reds (Cabernet Franc or youthful Rioja) with poultry or creamy dishes.
- Light, crisp whites (Pinot Grigio or Melon de Bourgogne/Muscadet) with salads or delicate fish.

CONTRASTING FLAVOUR INTENSITY

Sometimes contrasting depth or weight of flavour achieves a satisfying balance, particularly if the chosen wine brings life or freshness to the dish, such as:

- Citrusy, fresh white wines (unoaked Chardonnay or Picpoul de Pinet) with creamy dishes with depth, such as moules marinières or cheese soufflé.
- Light, fruit-forward red wines (Pinot Noir or Gamay) with rich, gamey dishes, such as duck confit.

WHEN CONTRAST DOESN'T WORK

On some occasions, too much contrast can lead to an imbalance, with either the wine or the dish drowning out the other. Some examples are:

- Steak with white wine – the wine can be overpowered by the richness of the meat.
- Blue cheese with light white wine – the wine can be overpowered by the strong flavour of blue cheese.
- Bold red wine with creamy and light cheeses – here the red wine can dominate the more delicate cheese flavours.
- Fresh salads with oaked, ripe Chardonnay (some Californian styles, for example) – as above, these styles of white wine will overwhelm crisp salads.

FLAVOUR SYNERGY

I love exploring flavour synergies between wines and recipes. It's one of my favourite aspects to play with, picking up on similar nuances between the plate and the glass.

Many grapes take on different, distinct flavours that arise naturally through fermentation and winemaking processes, as well as through ageing. We find many categories of flavour in wine: fruit, floral, herbaceous, spice, dairy, woody, baked and so on, so there are many strands to tease out in different dishes. Let's look at a few grape varieties and some of the common flavours (ingredients) that can be incorporated into a dish to create synergy. For more details of the flavours found in 20 key grape varieties, see pages 48–53 and 56–61.

- Pinot Noir – mushroom, cherry, cranberry
- Syrah – blackberry, black pepper, smoky
- Nebbiolo – mushroom, truffle, rose
- Sauvignon Blanc – lemon, asparagus, grass
- Riesling – mango, lime, blossom
- Oaked Chardonnay – lemon, light spice, creamy

TOUCH

Touch can play an exciting role when it comes to food and wine pairing. Here are some key aspects to consider in a wine:

Body – Consider whether to complement or contrast the body of a wine with the weight of a dish. For example, try complementing a rich bolognese with a full-bodied red wine, such as Chianti, or contrasting a creamy pasta with a light, fresh white wine, such as Muscadet.

Texture – Leaning into a white wine's buttery or creamy texture, or a red wine's plush and rounded texture, can create indulgent and satisfying pairings. For example, a buttery oaked Chardonnay with fish and beurre blanc, or a tomato-based stew with Malbec.

Bubbles – The fizz in sparkling wine brings an extra textural dimension that can be great fun when pairing with food. In particular, I love the contrast between the fresh prickle of bubbles and crunchy or fatty textures – such as fried food, creamy risotto and cheese – for intrigue and lift.

Tannins – It's important to consider the tannins in red wines when pairing them with food. As we've seen earlier in this chapter, umami, bitterness, spice and sweetness in food can increase our perception of tannins in wines, making them appear more grippy and drying.

Consider the nature of the tannins in the red wine you're serving. Are they:

- light and silky (as in many Pinot Noirs)
- smooth and velvety (as in some Malbec)
- fine but firm (as in many Syrahs)
- powerful and grippy (as found in classic Cabernet Sauvignon or Nebbiolo)?

And how will that sit alongside your proposed dish?

While pairing red wine with fish was once seen as the ultimate faux pas, reds with light, silky tannins can be a great fit – think Pinot Noir, Gamay (Beaujolais), Frappato, Cinsault or Barbera. By contrast, reds with higher tannins can interact poorly with fish and shellfish, often creating a bitter or metallic sensation.

TERROIR MATCHING

You may well be familiar with the expression 'what grows together, goes together' – a concept of food and wine pairing that really resonates with me, bringing it all back to place, or *terroir*.

The French word *terroir* refers to the unique combination of factors that define a place – its soil, climate, topography, and wider geographical and human context – and how these influence the character of the wine. *Terroir*-driven wines seek to capture the place they are from, and those who appreciate these wines value the nuances in the aromas, flavours and feel of a wine influenced by a particular place. You'll find lots of recipes in this book inspired by wines and ingredients found in the same location, that connect and feel harmonious in the most natural of ways. Some of the classic and best-known examples include:

- Tuscany – Sangiovese-based wines with tomatoes.
- Piedmont – Nebbiolo with white truffles from the woodlands.
- Loire – Sauvignon Blanc with local goats' cheese.
- Languedoc – Picpoul with oysters and mussels from nearby farms.
- Rías Baixas – Albariño with locally caught seafood and shellfish.
- Andalusia – Fino Sherry and Manzanilla with local anchovies, olives and jamón.
- California – Napa Cabernet Sauvignon with local beef.

EXPERIENCE

It's worth remembering that generally acknowledged principles, rules and ideas on food and wine pairing are by no means set in stone. Our palates and perception of taste, flavour and touch in wine and food are completely unique to our genetic make-up and lived experiences, so a group of guests may have a spectrum of different reference points when sharing the same food and wine. But isn't seeing how we individually react to the same sensory experience part of the pleasure?

I am one for experimenting and sometimes pushing boundaries with pairings. In true me fashion, sometimes I break the rules, pushing my palate to try something a little unexpected. Here are a few of my favourite less conventional pairings that bend the rules.

Red wine and fish – While diners have become more accustomed to light and silky reds with fish dishes, sometimes I'll pair a more robust style of red with fish. A particular favourite is anchovy pizza with a Rhône-style Syrah, as I love that briny, smoky quality shared across the two.

White wine and red meat – While I acknowledged earlier in this chapter that steak and white wine is generally not a good match given the imbalance of flavour intensity and body, I have had some gorgeously rich lamb dishes that have matched beautifully with rich styles of white wine. For example, a lamb and apricot tagine paired with a rich and perfumed Viognier with all that texture and those aromatics; and a slow-cooked Middle Eastern-spiced lamb shoulder with an aged, oaked white Rioja, again with powerful flavours and texture from oak to match the depth of the dish.

Fine wine and fast food – For me, the perception that fine wine should only be paired with high-end cuisine is a rule just meant to be broken! I simply adore a 'high-low' style of pairing – premium wine with humble food. Think Champagne or up-market Chardonnay with fish and chips, mac and cheese, or similar casual, fatty food delights. I also recall a wonderful reception I attended where the lusciously sweet (but with bracing acidity) Sauternes was served with fried chicken – that sweet, acidic, salty and crunchy pairing was the most moreish combination. Similarly, pizza, combining flavourful fresh tomato with a crunchy base and some fat from cheese, is wonderfully versatile for pairing with lighter high-quality reds, such as Pinot Noir, Frappato and approachable styles of Nebbiolo. Another favourite is a sweeter style of sparkling wine (from the higher-dosage end of Brut to Extra-Dry or Demi-Sec) with takeout curry. I like to skip the pretentiousness – there's no need to save fine wine for fine food.

Dry red wine and chocolate – This should be a no, but sometimes it is a yes from me. Fruit-forward styles of red wine containing light to medium tannins – mainly Pinot Noir, Gamay, or some lighter styles of Syrah – paired with dark (bittersweet) chocolate can work beautifully. Not because it's sweet on sweet, but because of the echo between fruit and earthy richness.

WHITE WINE WHEEL

This wheel broadly arranges white grape varieties from lightest to boldest in style and groups them by shared characteristics. It's a useful starting point for food pairing, helping us to consider how a wine's weight, intensity and character sit alongside the different elements of a dish.

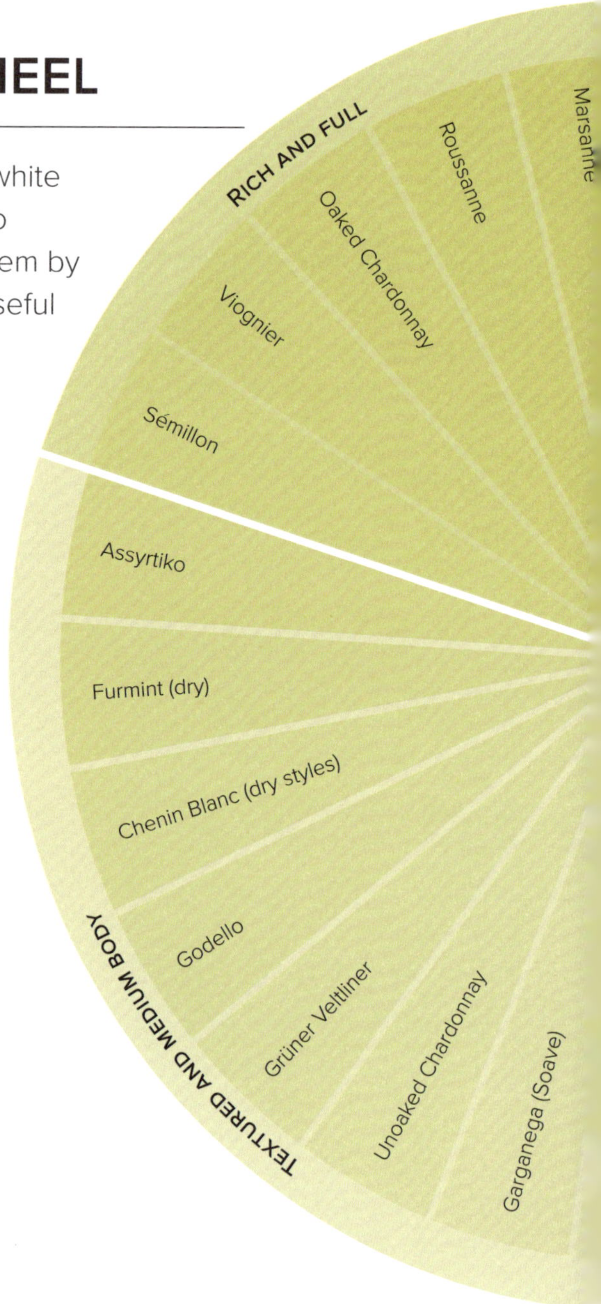

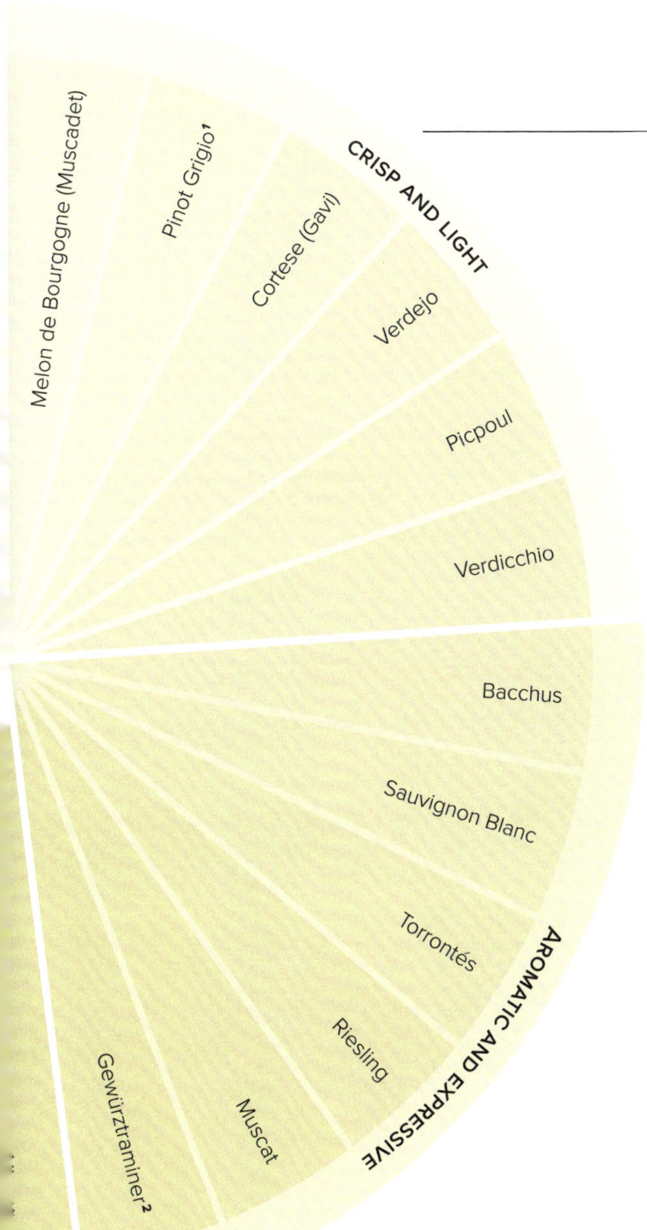

[1] Can be made into a richer style, like those from Alsace.
[2] Can be made into a very rich and full style.

QUICK GUIDE TO PAIRING FOOD WITH WHITE WINES

Let's look at the flavour profiles and styles of ten of the world's most popular white grapes, and consider the key pairing principles and the most successful food matches for each grape variety, along with

Grape	Profile and Styles	Key Regions
Chardonnay	From lean, unoaked styles with citrus and mineral freshness to fuller, oaked expressions with stone fruit, tropical notes and a creamy texture. Typically high in acidity. Also used in sparkling wines, either blended or as Blanc de Blancs.	France: Chablis, Côte de Beaune, Mâconnais, Champagne; USA: California, Oregon; Australia: Yarra Valley, Margaret River; Chile; South Africa; England.
Sauvignon Blanc	Zesty and aromatic with piercing acidity. Cooler regions impart citrus, mineral and grassy notes, while warmer climates show tropical fruit, such as passionfruit and melon.	France: Sancerre, Pouilly-Fumé, Bordeaux; New Zealand: Marlborough.
Riesling	Brisk acidity and expressive aromatics, from citrus and green apple to mango and blossom. Style ranges from bone-dry to lusciously sweet.	Germany: Mosel; France: Alsace; Australia: Clare and Eden Valleys; USA: Finger Lakes.

suggested recipes from this book that will pair with beautifully with these wines.

Pairing Principles	Food Matches	Recipes
High acidity cuts through fat and enhances umami. Unoaked styles suit delicate textures, while richer styles complement creamier, fuller dishes.	From raw or simply cooked seafood, poultry and salads to richer lobster thermidor, creamy poultry and fish, roasted veg and cheese.	✦ Champagne with fish goujons, devilled eggs and caviar (see page 73) ✦ Lightly oaked Chardonnay with mini crab brioche buns (see page 77) ✦ Chablis with scallops and samphire (see page 90) ✦ Oaked Chardonnay with halibut and a lumpfish roe butter sauce (see page 109) ✦ Champagne with mac and cheese (see page 165)
High acidity and bold, fresh flavours suit similarly vibrant dishes, especially those with vegetable, herbaceous (and even bitter) nuance and aromatic spice.	Goats' cheese, herby veggie dishes, green salads, fresh fish or light poultry.	✦ Sauvignon Blanc with a veggie platter and whipped feta dip (see page 78) ✦ Sauvignon Blanc with pea and asparagus frittata (see page 154)
Bright acidity lifts fresh dishes. Off-dry and sweet styles balance spice and intense flavours. Sweet styles pair with fruit desserts.	Salads, cured and raw fish, aromatic curries, spicy salads and fruit-forward, citrusy desserts.	✦ Dry Riesling with sea bass crudo (see page 101) ✦ Off-dry Riesling with spicy prawn noodle salad (see page 102) ✦ Off-dry Riesling with one-pot green curry (see page 124)

QUICK GUIDE TO PAIRING FOOD WITH WHITE WINES

Grape	Profile and Styles	Key Regions
Chenin Blanc	Ranges from light and appley to rich and textured with ripe orchard fruit, floral lift and earthy undertones. Usually backed by fresh acidity. Made dry to sweet, still to sparkling, and oaked.	France: Loire Valley; South Africa: Swartland.
Pinot Grigio/ Gris	From light and easy drinking – apple, lemon, stony – to richer, spiced styles with stone fruit and honey.	Italy: Northeast for simple styles, Alto Adige for premium; France: Alsace (Pinot Gris).
Albariño	Bright and citrusy with zippy acidity, peachy fruit and a saline edge.	Spain: Rías Baixas.
Viognier	Rich, perfumed and textured, with peach, white flowers, spice and hints of citrus peel or honey.	France: Condrieu, Northern Rhône; USA; Australia.

Pairing Principles	Food Matches	Recipes
Easy-drinking styles suit simple dishes. Richer styles match umami and spice, while acidity balances fat and sweetness. Sweet styles pair with fruit desserts and pastry.	Salads, root veg – pumpkin or squash, roast chicken or pork belly, and dishes with fragrant spice or sweetness from fruit, honey and sugars.	✦ Chenin Blanc with chicken, tarragon and pears (see page 128) ✦ Chenin Blanc with honey and miso pork belly (see page 139)
Lighter styles for gentle flavours. Richer or off-dry styles suit spice, fruit or sweetness.	Grilled veg, salads, fresh cheeses, such as mozzarella or ricotta, light pastas or aromatic tagines.	✦ Pinot Grigio with grilled peach, pine nut and ricotta salad (see page 158)
Acidity and texture make it great for fresh seafood, as well as fattier dishes.	Prawns (shrimp), clams, mussels – especially with lemon. Creamy seafood or chicken, and fried snacks.	✦ Albariño with clams in white wine (see page 93)
Bold enough for rich, umami dishes and handles sweet spice well.	Roast chicken, pumpkin or squash, fragrant tagines.	✦ Viognier with chicken and pumpkin pie (see page 127)

QUICK GUIDE TO PAIRING FOOD WITH WHITE WINES

Grape	Profile and Styles	Key Regions
Grüner Veltliner	Lemony, crisp and peppery with vegetal notes, such as celery and radish, stone fruit and a bright streak of acidity.	Austria: Wachau.
Melon de Bourgogne	Crisp and light, with lemon, apple and delicate floral notes, plus a saline freshness.	France: Loire Valley (Muscadet).
Garganega	Rounded texture with fresh acidity, and flavours of apple, pear, stone fruit, delicate florals and subtle almond or nutty hints.	Italy: Soave.

Pairing Principles	Food Matches	Recipes
Fresh, peppery, herbal profile suits dishes that echo its flavours. Its acidity makes it great with fried foods.	Vegetable and herb-led dishes, simply cooked fish or chicken, fried snacks such as tempura or chicken goujons.	✦ Grüner Veltliner with a herby trout salad (see page 110)
Refreshing citrus and delicate flavours pair best with similarly subtle, freshly prepared dishes.	Simply prepared fish and shellfish, such as plateau de fruits de mer, smoked salmon or sushi.	✦ Muscadet with dressed crab, a pint of prawns (shrimp) and chips (see page 94)
The subtle flavour and rounded texture but present acidity pair well with medium-intensity dishes, especially those with cream or a nutty richness.	Pasta with seafood or chicken, risottos, nutty vegetarian recipes.	✦ Soave with pesto pasta (see page 153)

RED WINE WHEEL

As with the white wine wheel, this wheel broadly arranges red grape varieties from lightest to boldest in style, and groups them by shared characteristics. It's a useful starting point for food pairing, helping you to consider how a wine's weight, intensity and character sit alongside the different elements of a dish.

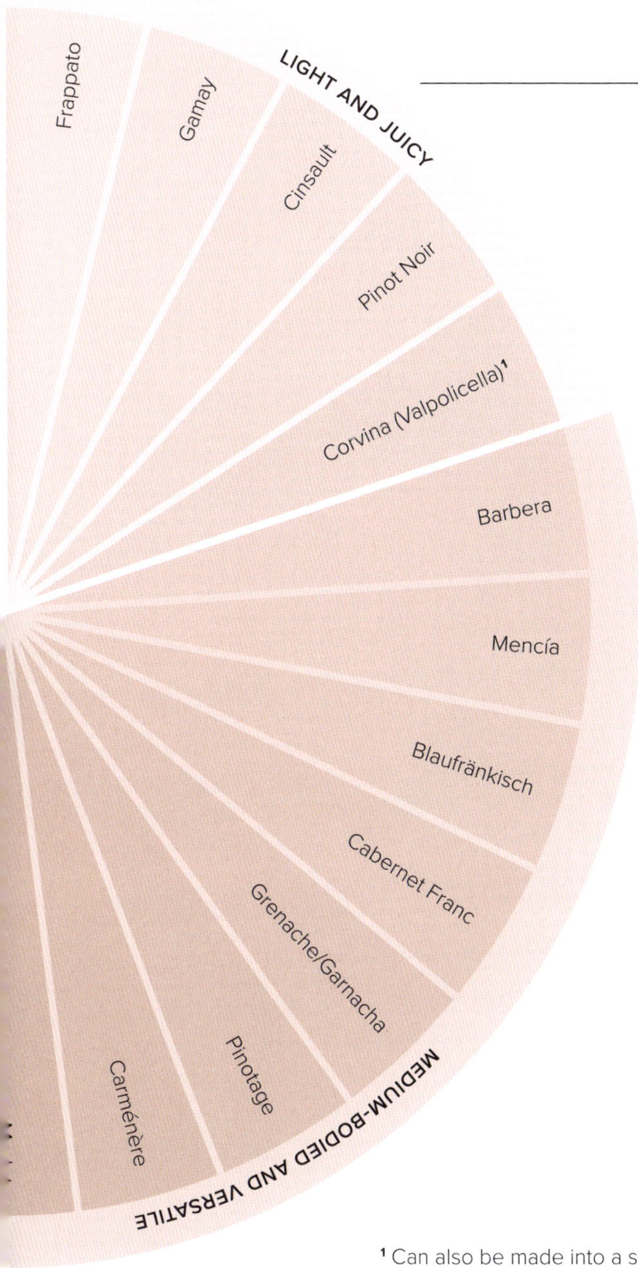

[1] Can also be made into a sweeter, full-bodied and powerful style, gaining concentration through the process of drying.

QUICK GUIDE TO PAIRING FOOD WITH RED WINES

Here we look at the flavour profiles and styles of ten of the world's most popular red grapes, and consider the key pairing principles and the most successful food matches for each grape variety. There

Grape	Profile and Styles	Key Regions
Cabernet Sauvignon	Full-bodied and structured, firm tannins and high acidity. Classic flavours include blackcurrant, graphite, mint, eucalyptus and green bell pepper, toasty and clove notes from oak. As it matures, leathery, tobacco and coffee notes emerge.	France: Bordeaux (especially the Left Bank); USA: Napa Valley; Australia: Coonawarra and Margaret River; South Africa: Stellenbosch.
Pinot Noir	Light to medium in body with fine, smooth tannins, high acidity, and a red fruit character – cherry, raspberry. With age it gains earthy, savoury depth, plus notes of mushroom and autumnal leaves. Oak use can give spice.	France: Burgundy (especially Côte de Nuits); USA: Oregon and California; New Zealand: Central Otago; Germany; Australia.
Syrah	Medium to full-bodied with high tannin and acidity, ranges from cool-climate styles – peppery, floral and savoury with dark fruit and smoke – to richer, riper styles with jammy fruit, a plush texture and warming spice.	France: Northern Rhône (Côte-Rôtie, Hermitage, Cornas); Australia: Barossa and the cooler Victoria; USA: Paso Robles.

are also suggested recipes from this book that will pair successfully with these wines.

Pairing Principles	Food Matches	Recipes
Bold flavours, high tannins and acidity make Cabernet Sauvignon ideal for rich, umami-forward dishes and those with fat and texture/structure. Salty dishes soften its tannins.	Best with red meats, such as steak, beef Wellington or braised beef pie. Pair with rich, mushroom-based dishes, such as stroganoff, or hard cheeses, such as aged Cheddar.	✦ Cabernet Sauvignon with steak, red wine butter and marrow (see page 143)
Its bright acidity and savoury depth make it great with umami-rich dishes and those with some fat; lighter styles suit more delicate flavours and textures.	Duck and game, mushroom and truffle dishes. Lighter styles also pair well with oily fish, such as seared tuna or salmon with Mediterranean vegetables. Suits fragrant spices, such as clove, cinnamon and star anise.	✦ Pinot Noir with confit duck, blood orange and sweet potato (see page 131)
Bold flavour and structure suit intense, smoky, spiced or umami-rich dishes. Present acidity and tannin also cut through fat.	Great with smoky barbecue meats, lamb, game and smoky vegetables, such as grilled aubergine (eggplant) and mushrooms.	✦ Syrah with smoky short rib (see page 144)

QUICK GUIDE TO PAIRING FOOD WITH RED WINES

Grape	Profile and Styles	Key Regions
Tempranillo	Medium to full-bodied, with moderate to firm tannins and fresh acidity, red cherry and plum along with savoury notes of tomato, herbs and spice. Oak can add vanilla and coconut, while bottle age brings leather, earth and tobacco.	Spain: Rioja and Ribera del Duero.
Malbec	Full and generous, with velvety tannins and moderate acidity. Expect bold flavours of blackberry and plum, floral notes such as violet, and cocoa, smoke or spice in richer styles.	Agentina: Mendoza; France: originally from Cahors.
Sangiovese	High acidity and grainy tannins, with cherry and plum alongside savoury tomato, dried herbs and earth. Oak adds cedar or clove, while age can bring leather and balsamic depth.	Italy: Tuscany, especially the regions of Chianti and Brunello di Montalcino.

Pairing Principles	Food Matches	Recipes
Medium to full-bodied, with tannin and acidity present, making it a versatile match for a range of umami-rich and Mediterranean dishes.	Youthful styles pair well with tapas, tomato-based poultry or meat dishes, and grilled veg. Aged styles suit richer poultry or red meats, or fragrant, peppery dishes, such as black pepper beef.	✦ Red Rioja with Mediterranean chicken (see page 123)
Generous texture and rich fruit make it easy to pair with hearty, flavourful dishes and foods with full texture.	Classic with steak and barbecue meats. Also great with tomato-based dishes, root veg, meaty pizzas or smoky veg-based recipes.	✦ Malbec with smash burger and plum ketchup (see page 147)
Suits dishes with richness and layered textures. Cuts through fat and pairs well with salty cheese	Pair with tomato-based pasta or meat dishes, rich lamb or duck, or salty cheeses, such as Pecorino.	✦ Sangiovese with duck ragu and pappardelle (see page 135)

QUICK GUIDE TO PAIRING FOOD WITH RED WINES

Grape	Profile and Styles	Key Regions
Grenache/ Garnacha	Plush and ripe, Grenache has low tannins and moderate acidity. Flavours range from vibrant red fruits and spice to fuller styles with stewed fruit, fruitcake and sweet spice warmth.	France: Southern Rhône – Châteauneuf-du-Pape, blended in Côtes du Rhône; Spain: Priorat, Gredos; Australia; USA.
Nebbiolo	Perfumed and earthy with high tannins and acidity, offering red cherry, rose, violet and tar. With age, it develops truffle, leather and earthy complexity.	Italy: Piedmont, especially Barolo, Barbaresco and the wider Langhe region.
Cabernet Franc	Medium-bodied with tart red fruits, such as cranberry and raspberry, floral notes, stony earthiness, and a leafy or green bell pepper note.	France: Loire Valley (Chinon, Saumur-Champigny), Bordeaux (typically blended); USA; Canada; Italy.
Gamay	Light and juicy, lively acidity, low tannins, bright red fruits, such as strawberry and raspberry. In *Cru* (named vilage) styles, layers of floral, earthy or granite-like character. Some very light styles show a banana or candyfloss nuance.	France: Beaujolais – renowned *Crus* include Fleurie, Morgon and Brouilly.

Pairing Principles	Food Matches	Recipes
Lighter styles suit softer, mid-weight dishes; bolder styles match richly flavoured or slow-cooked meats.	Lighter styles pair with oily fish or structured dishes, such as monkfish, poultry or duck with red fruit. Fuller styles suit lamb, pork or spiced, slow-cooked meat dishes.	✦ Garnacha with warm duck salad (see page 132)
Its high tannin and acidity work well with rich, umami or fatty dishes, and those with texture. Salt softens its tannins.	Ideal with truffle and mushrooms, game meats and rich beef dishes such, as steak or braised beef.	✦ Nebbiolo with mushroom and truffle tagliatelle (see page 157)
Medium body, acidity and green savoury edge make it flexible with veg-forward and umami dishes, as well as a range of medium-intense dishes.	Great with pork, lamb chops, grilled veg, mushrooms, ratatouille or herby poultry dishes.	✦ Cabernet Franc with pork and Padron pepper kebabs (see page 136)
Lighter styles suit snacks and fish, juicier styles can cut through fat and mild spice, while more complex styles match richer and umami-forward dishes.	Salty aperitivo snacks, baked salmon and other medium-intense fish or seafood dishes. Great with poultry, duck or mildly spiced dishes, such as aromatic curries, Chinese spices.	✦ Beaujolais with cheese and meat board (see page 186)

PAIRING FOOD WITH SPARKLING AND ROSÉ WINES

This section focuses on the key styles of sparkling and rosé wines, with pairing principles, complementary dishes and suggested recipes from this book.

SPARKLING WINES

STYLES

Traditional-method sparkling wines are made with a second fermentation, where the wine spends extended time in contact with the lees (used yeast cells) in the bottle. This gives brioche and pastry-style notes, which sit alongside flavours of citrus and orchard fruit, and usually high acidity. In the tank method, used notably for Prosecco, this process takes place more quickly, so these wines tend to have a fresher, simpler and fruity character, typically of lemon and pear. *Pétillant naturel* or *méthode ancestrale* sparkling wines undergo just one fermentation in the bottle – they're unfiltered, lightly fizzy, often cloudy, fruity and usually lower in alcohol.

Sparkling wines vary from bone-dry to sweet, with most falling in the categories of Brut Nature, Extra Brut, Brut and Extra Dry. They can be made from just white grapes (Blanc de Blancs), just red grapes (Blanc de Noirs) or from a blend of red and white grapes (rosé or pink). They can be made in a fresher or richer style (the latter typically attributed to extended lees ageing and sometimes oak contact), and from a single vintage or multi vintages (referred to as 'non-vintage'). Some are suitable for extensive bottle ageing and can develop honey, nutty and earthy notes.

KEY REGIONS

France: Champagne and Crémant; Spain: Cava and Corpinnat; England; Italy: Franciacorta, Trento, Prosecco; South Africa: Méthode Cap Classique; Germany; Australia: Tasmania; USA: California.

PAIRING PRINCIPLES AND FOOD MATCHES

High acidity cuts through fat (think crispy snacks, fish and chips) and enhances umami (particularly fish, shellfish and mushroom). Fresher styles (usually non-vintage, traditional-method sparkling wines or Prosecco) tend to suit more subtle flavours (raw and cured fish, salads), while richer styles of traditional-method sparkling (extended lees ageing, oak contact, vintage styles) complement richer, creamier, umami-forward dishes (poultry and fish with creamy sauces, cheese, truffle). Styles with more sweetness can balance spice (mild to medium curries and tagines).

RECIPES

- ✦ Champagne with fish goujons (see page 73)
- ✦ Cava with truffled cheese toasties (see page 74)
- ✦ Sparkling rosé with beef carpaccio, truffle mayo and mushrooms (see page 140)
- ✦ Champagne with mac and cheese (see page 165)

ROSÉ WINES

STYLES

Good-quality styles of rosé range from pale-coloured with subtle fruit notes (citrus, stone fruit, berries, melon) and stony, mineral notes, to darker-hued wines with more pronounced berry notes, similar mineral hints and sometimes herbs and spice, depending on the varieties used. Most are unoaked and made for consuming within a couple of years of being made (with some exceptions). Most quality rosés are made just from red grapes, with the depth of colour depending on how long the grape skins (which contain colour pigment) are in contact with the pulp and juice during the winemaking process.

KEY REGIONS

France: Provence, Languedoc, Rhône Valley and the Loire; Spain: Navarra and Rioja; Italy; USA; South Africa.

PAIRING PRINCIPLES AND FOOD MATCHES

Many styles display fresh acidity and light to medium body, with subtle to more pronounced fruit flavours, so have depth and freshness, giving them versatility to pair with a range of dishes. Lighter styles with nuanced fruit pair well with fresh dishes (salads, Mediterranean vegetables and herbs, fresh and cured seafood), umami ingredients (fresh shellfish with lemon) and light and fatty dishes (creamy dishes, fried snacks). Those styles with more depth (usually the dry, darker-hued picks) can stand up to more robust flavours (rich tomato-based sauces, poultry and duck, and even simply grilled meats, such as herby barbecue lamb chops). The berry fruit nuances in rosé can make it a great pairing with aromatic, fragrant and lightly spiced dishes too, with the berry fruit balancing the spices.

RECIPES

- ✦ Rosé with beetroot-and-gin-cured salmon (see page 85)
- ✦ Deep-hued rosé with tuna niçoise (see page 113)
- ✦ Provence rosé with spicy salmon skewers (see page 114)

PAIRING FOOD WITH SWEET WINES

This section turns to sweet wines, offering guidance on pairing approaches, delicious food matches and recommended recipes from this book.

SWEET WINES

STYLES

Sweetness is the amount of sugar in a wine, typically referred to as residual sugar, and is best detected on the finish of a wine. Sweet wines can range from off-dry, with a small amount of detectable sweetness, to lusciously sweet, with extremely high levels. They come in many styles: red, white, rosé, still, sparkling and fortified. Sweet wines can be made in a number of ways, but quality sweet wines are typically achieved in one of these two ways:

- **Concentrating natural grape sugars**, as seen in:
    - Botrytis-affected grapes (also known as noble rot), such as Sauternes
    - Late-harvest grapes, common for some Riesling and Chenin Blanc
    - Drying grapes, as in Amarone della Valpolicella
    - Freezing grapes, as in German Eiswein or Canadian ice wine
- **Stopping the fermentation**, which prevents all the natural sugars from being fermented into alcohol. This can be done through fortification, as for example in Port (see page 66).

Here is a summary of the terms winemakers use to describe sweet wine:

- **Off-dry wines** A small amount of sweetness
- **Medium-dry to medium-sweet wines** Present sweetness
- **Sweet wines** Distinctive sweetness
- **Lusciously sweet** Extremely high levels of sweetness

KEY REGIONS

France: Sauternes; Côteaux du Layon, Vouvray and other Loire Valley appellations; Vin Doux Naturel wines from the Languedoc, Roussillon and Rhône Valley; and select Alsace wines labelled Vendanges Tardives or Sélection de Grains Nobles; Germany: Certain sweet Rieslings; Portugal: Madeira and Port; Italy: Moscato d'Asti; Hungary: Tokaji; Spain: Sherry (notably Pedro Ximénez and Moscatel); Canada: Icewine.

PAIRING PRINCIPLES AND FOOD MATCHES

Sweet foods are best paired with wines that are equally sweet, as sweetness can make dry wines taste bitter and accentuate acidity. The most successful sweet wine and food pairings also consider acidity in both the wine and the dish, to create balance.

It's also helpful to think about the flavour intensity and texture of a wine when pairing with dessert – delicate, light and fruity desserts, such as fruit sorbets, work best with similarly textured sweet wines (such as Moscato d'Asti), while richer, heavier desserts suit fuller-bodied sweet wines (certain Ports, for example – see page 66). It's also worth considering the satisfying flavour combinations of sweet wines with salty foods, especially blue cheese (see more on pages 14–15), and sweet wines with spicy food (see more on pages 30–1). For more classic sweet food and sweet wine pairings, see page 27.

RECIPES

- Sauternes with griddled pineapple, ice cream and honeyed nuts (see page 175)
- Tokaji with apricot tarte Tatin (see page 176)
- Moscato d'Asti with white chocolate rainbow bark (see page 179)
- Off-dry Riesling with one-pot green curry (see page 124)
- Off-dry Riesling with spicy prawn noodle salad (see page 102)

PAIRING FOOD WITH FORTIFED AND ORANGE WINES

This section explores orange and fortified wines, with matching guidelines, suggestions for great plates to enjoy alongside these wines and featured recipes from this book.

FORTIFIED WINES

STYLES

Fortified wines have additional alcohol added during production, typically reaching 15–22% ABV. When pairing them with food, consider whether they're made from white or red grapes, their flavour intensity, and whether they're dry or sweet. Styles range from bone-dry (Fino and Manzanilla Sherry) to lusciously sweet (ruby Port, Pedro Ximénez Sherry). Some are best enjoyed young (Fino, ruby Port), while others age for years before release and can improve further in the bottle (Colheita Port, vintage Port, aged tawny Port, Rutherglen Muscat).

Certain styles are aged under a layer of yeast (flor), giving a tangy, savoury character (Fino and Manzanilla Sherry), while others mature oxidatively in barrel, developing nutty richness (Amontillado and Oloroso Sherry, Bual and Sercial Madeira, tawny Port). Some are light, fresh and crisp (Fino and Manzanilla Sherry), while others are full-bodied and intensely flavoured (Pedro Ximénez Sherry, vintage Port, Rutherglen Muscat).

KEY REGIONS

Spain: Sherry; Portugal: Port and Madeira; France: Vin Doux Naturel; Australia: Rutherglen Muscat.

PAIRING PRINCIPLES AND FOOD MATCHES

Light, dry and fresh styles of Sherry suit similarly intense dishes – try pairing Fino Sherry with fish and light tapas. Those styles with more intensity can stand up to richer flavours, such as Amontillado Sherry with meaty stews and umami-forward recipes. Very rich and sweet styles of Sherry, as well as red/ruby or tawny Port (which is always sweet to varying levels) can work well with salty or blue cheeses and a range of desserts, particularly those with dark (bittersweet) chocolate (ruby or tawny Port), those with pastry (tawny Port) or rich and creamy desserts (Pedro Ximenez Sherry). Madeira from Portugal goes well with treacle tart or other nutty, rich, molasses-based desserts.

RECIPES

- Dry Sherry with jamón ibérico, anchovies and olives (see page 81)
- Tawny Port with rocky road (see page 172)

ORANGE WINES

STYLES

Orange wines can range from a light golden hue to a deep amber colour, and every shade of orange in between. They are made from white grapes, with the depth of the colour usually indicating the length of time the grape skins have been in contact with the juice and pulp. Lighter-hued styles usually undergo anything from a day to a couple of weeks of skin contact, while deeper-hued styles may undergo up to several months. Those deeper-hued styles will have more texture from the tannins extracted from the grape skins. They can display a variety of flavours, such as citrus peel, stone fruits, honey and nuts, perfume and spices, and can have a savoury-umami – almost salty – character.

KEY REGIONS

Georgia; Italy; Slovenia.

PAIRING PRINCIPLES AND FOOD MATCHES

Lighter styles suit softer, mid-weight dishes, whereas bolder styles, usually with more texture, can match more richly flavoured dishes with roundness. The savoury-umami, almost salty, character can be drawn out and mirrored in similar ingredients and dishes, such as root vegetables, cured meats and cheese for a harmonious match. Again, dishes using herbs and spices can echo similar notes in the orange wines, creating unity between wine and dish.

RECIPES

- Orange wine with spiced chickpeas, saucisson and grilled artichokes (see page 82)
- Orange wine with fried gnocchi, sage and butternut (see page 161)

PART 2

PAIR

APÉRO, BOARDS & NIBBLES

Champagne with fish goujons, devilled eggs and caviar 73

Cava with truffled cheese toasties 74

Lightly oaked Chardonnay with mini crab brioche buns 77

Sauvignon Blanc with a veggie platter and whipped feta dip 78

Dry Sherry with jamón ibérico, anchovies and olives 81

Orange wine with spiced chickpeas, saucisson and grilled artichokes 82

Rosé with beetroot-and-gin-cured salmon 85

Beaujolais with cheese and meat board 86

Champagne with fish goujons, devilled eggs and caviar

SERVES 4

For the devilled eggs

6 eggs

2–3 tablespoons mayonnaise

1 teaspoon Dijon mustard

¼ teaspoon smoked paprika

salt and pepper

finely chopped chives, to garnish

For the fish goujons

75g (2¾oz) plain flour (all-purpose flour)

2 eggs, beaten

100g (3½oz) panko breadcrumbs

250g (9oz) boneless, skinless cod fillet, cut into fingers

vegetable oil, for shallow-frying

To serve

caviar or lumpfish caviar

aioli

Let's start with a 'high-low' style of pairing – fine wine and simple snacks (with a side of caviar) – where a little decadence and glamour meet easy hosting. This is such a gorgeously indulgent way to start an evening and will impress your guests. We've got umami, salt and fat in these nibbles – the crunchy goujons, creamy eggs, briny caviar – so the ultimate pairing is Champagne. It matches flavour intensity, brings a savoury edge with its bready, saline notes, gives lift and lightness with its high acidity, and adds extra textural excitement with the bubbles.

For the devilled eggs, cook the eggs in boiling water for 8–10 minutes, before plunging into iced water to cool. Gently peel them, cut in half and scoop the yolks into a bowl. Combine the yolks with the mayonnaise, mustard and paprika, and season to taste. Pipe the mixture back into the whites, or carefully use a spoon. Sprinkle with the chives.

For the goujons, place the flour in one bowl and season to taste, place the eggs in another bowl and the breadcrumbs in a third. Dip the fish pieces in the flour to coat, tapping off the excess, then in the eggs, then the breadcrumbs. Heat the oil in a deep-sided frying pan until a crumb sizzles. Fry the goujons until cooked through and golden on both sides.

Place the caviar and aioli in bowls and serve alongside the eggs and goujons.

OTHER WINES

Traditional-method sparkling wines. Oaked Chardonnay from Burgundy or cooler regions of California (Sonoma Coast, Santa Barbara), Oregon, Australia (Yarra Valley, Mornington Peninsula), New Zealand (Auckland) and South Africa (Hemel-en-Aarde).

Cava with truffled cheese toasties

SERVES 4

200g (7oz) Manchego cheese, grated

200g (7oz) Cheddar cheese, grated

½ teaspoon black pepper

8 slices of quality sourdough bread

75g (2¾oz) butter

1 tablespoon good-quality truffle oil, plus extra for drizzling

guindilla peppers from a jar, to serve

I discovered this pairing in a Spanish wine bar in the hilltop village of Begur on the Costa Brava. It brings together a few of life's best things – melted cheese, truffle and bubbles. It's spot-on with Cava, as many styles show an earthy, graphite edge – thanks to the native Xarel·lo grape – which aligns beautifully with the savoury, foresty character of truffle. Pick a quality bottle with depth (look for *Reserva* or above for quality) and a dry style (*Brut Nature* or *Extra Brut* on the label). This match is all about richness, umami, salt and toasty intensity, balanced by bubbles and acidity for lift, cut and contrast.

Combine the cheeses and black pepper in a bowl.

Lightly toast one side of each slice of sourdough in a dry frying pan over medium heat. Place 4 slices, toasted side up, on a board and divide the cheese mixture between them. Press the remaining slices on top, toasted side down.

Melt the butter in a frying pan on a low-medium heat, adding the truffle oil as it bubbles. Gently cook the sandwiches until the cheese has melted, flipping halfway through cooking, until crisp and golden. Cut up and serve with the pickled peppers and an extra drizzle of truffle oil.

OTHER WINES

Try Corpinnat (breakaway appellation of top Spanish producers of traditional-method sparkling wines, leaning on native grapes, such as Xarel·lo). For still wines, try aged white Rioja, oaked Chardonnay or Jura Savagnin.

Lightly oaked Chardonnay with mini crab brioche buns

SERVES 4

8 mini brioche buns, halved

2 tablespoons salted butter, softened

250g (9oz) white crab meat

2 tablespoons mayonnaise

1 tablespoon finely chopped chives

zest and juice of ½ lemon, plus extra for squeezing

Baby Gem lettuce, shredded

Tabasco (optional)

salt and pepper

This takes me back to childhood holidays in Devon – crabs caught fresh that morning, dropped off at pubs, cracked and picked, then sandwiched with lashings of lemon and a dollop of mayo. Back then it was lemonade on the side, but my, what an upgrade a good white wine makes. For this elevated apéro look, I'm skipping the brown bread and using mini brioche buns. Lightly oaked Chardonnay – like those from the Mâconnais – is a great match. The buttery and oak flavours mirrors the richness of brioche, the soft texture echoes the crab, and the ripe fruit works in harmony with its slight sweetness. There's citrus, freshness and enough acidity to cut through the fat and umami in the filling.

Slice the mini brioche buns horizontally and butter the cut sides. Gently toast in a dry frying pan, butter sides down, until golden, then remove from the pan.

In a bowl, gently combine the crab, mayonnaise, chives, lemon zest and juice and season to taste.

Divide the filling between the bun, then add shredded lettuce, an extra squeeze of lemon, extra cracked pepper and Tabasco to taste.

OTHER WINES

Cool-climate lightly oaked Chardonnay, such as those from England and Tasmania, Australia. Textural, unoaked whites, such as Soave, or some styles of Albariño. Traditional-method sparkling wines.

Sauvignon Blanc with a veggie platter and whipped feta dip

SERVES 4

100g (3½oz) feta cheese

100g (3½oz) full-fat Greek yogurt

juice of ½ small lemon

¼ teaspoon black pepper

2 tablespoons olive oil

To serve

cucumber, chopped

asparagus, lightly steamed and cooled

fine green beans, lightly steamed and cooled

peas in shells

heritage carrots

baby tomatoes

mixed peppers, sliced

radishes

chicory (endive) leaves

This pairing is all about vibrancy, colour and freshness – in both the wine and the board. The result: an almost-too-chic-to-eat crudités platter that's just the ticket for a summery afternoon or golden hour aperitif. A classic, crisp Loire-style Sauvignon Blanc, balancing citrus fruit, subtle grassiness and mineral purity, is my pick. It pairs beautifully with the subtle flavour of raw veg, handles their bitter edge with ease, and brings a herby, green-on-green synergy. The whipped feta adds a salty tang that reflects the wine's zingy acidity, and together, the whole dish brings crispness, crunch and lifted flavour.

For the dip, blend all the ingredients in a small food processor until the desired consistency – I prefer something whipped and creamy. Alternatively, mash by hand with a fork for a coarser texture.

Place the feta dip on a large chopping board or plate. Fan piles of the different vegetables around it, varying colours and textures for a stylish and organic look.

OTHER WINES

Unoaked fresh and herby white wines, such as Grüner Veltliner, Bacchus or Verdejo. Light and delicate sparklings with a little sweetness, such as Prosecco, can work too. Also try dry, mineral-driven rosé wines, such as those from Provence.

Dry Sherry with jamón ibérico, anchovies and olives

SERVES 6

90g (3¼oz) anchovies

180g (6½oz) jamón ibérico

180–200g (6½–7oz) olives, drained

Anyone can fall in love with Sherry if you keep it simple. Start with the most accessible styles – Fino or Manzanilla (the latter is a specific type of Fino from Sanlúcar de Barrameda) – fridge-chilled and served with salty, savoury snacks. Five minutes of grazing and sipping should convert even the most reluctant of Sherry fans. These dry styles look like white wine, but taste distinct: tangy, saline, with a light nuttiness, a faint herby and floral edge and a mouth-watering finish. They come alive alongside anchovies, jamón and olives – a spread rich in salt, umami, fat and flavour intensity. The Sherry cuts through it all and links beautifully with its Andalusian roots.

Anchovies – My pick is fresh anchovies marinated in vinegar, perhaps with a little parsley: fresh, simple and tangy like the Sherry. One of my greatest wine moments was tasting Manzanilla straight from the cask in its hometown, Sanlúcar de Barrameda, while tucking into local boquerones en vinagre. Pure terroir magic.

Jamón – The best is 100 per cent Ibérico de Bellota, the fattiest, nuttiest style with the greatest depth of flavour. It's melt-in-the-mouth deliciousness, classified under a black label, and comes with a price tag to match. Next in the hierarchy is red label jamón (50–75 per cent Ibérico de Bellota) – a little less intense but still superb quality and more affordable.

Olives – For added terroir matching, go for Manzanilla olives, which, like Sherry, are also from Andalusia. They're a little meaty, subtly briny and nutty, and pick up on many of the same savoury qualities that you find in Fino and Manzanilla styles.

OTHER WINES

Keeping on the Spanish theme, I'd pick a very crisp, dry style of Cava (look for Brut Nature on the label) or a fresh and spritzy Txakoli from Basque Country.

Orange wine with spiced chickpeas, saucisson and grilled artichokes

SERVES 4–6

400g (14oz) can chickpeas in water, rinsed and drained

¼ teaspoon ground turmeric

1 teaspoon ground cumin

1 teaspoon dried oregano

pinch of cayenne pepper

zest of ½ lemon

½ teaspoon flaky sea salt

2 tablespoons olive oil

1 saucisson, sliced into 5mm (¼ inch) pieces

black pepper

For the grilled artichokes

400g (14oz) can artichoke hearts in water, drained

juice of ½ lemon

½ teaspoon flaky sea salt

1 tablespoon olive oil

½ teaspoon smoked paprika (optional)

OTHER WINES

Rich, perfumed, textured white wines, such as Rhône-style whites: Marsanne-Roussanne blends, Grenache Blanc and Viognier. Fruity and light styles of Garnacha.

Orange wines are a great match for the umami-rich, fatty and fragrant ingredients in this apéro plate. My pick is a light-coloured orange – generally, the paler the hue, the gentler the tannins and less intense the flavour, making it easier drinking for this kind of spread. Tannin, colour and flavour all come from the grape skins in orange winemaking, so lighter often means smoother and more approachable. These wines can show a perfumed, lifted bouquet – citrus peel, stone fruit, spice and earthy-savoury undertones – giving them a kind of umami character. Their gentle grip pairs brilliantly with oily textures, salt and spice. Served lightly chilled, they're a characterful apéro pick that'll get everyone talking – just don't chill too cold, or you might risk muting their perfume and exaggerating their bitterness.

Preheat the oven to 200°C (180°C fan), 400°F, Gas Mark 6.

Pat the chickpeas dry on kitchen paper and place in a bowl with the spices, lemon zest, salt and oil. Toss well to coat, then spread in a single layer on a baking tray. Bake for 20 minutes, shaking halfway through, until crisp and golden.

Pat the artichokes dry and toss them with the lemon juice, salt, oil and smoked paprika, if using. Heat a griddle pan or frying pan until hot – the artichokes should sizzle when they hit the pan – and cook for a few minutes on each side until golden.

Place the chickpeas and artichokes in separate bowls, sprinkle with an extra pinch of flaky sea salt and black pepper and serve warm or cold with the saucisson.

Rosé with beetroot-and-gin-cured salmon

SERVES 6

100g (3½oz) raw beetroot, peeled and cut into chunks

75g (2¾oz) coarse sea salt

75g (2¾oz) golden caster sugar (superfine sugar)

1 teaspoon black pepper

zest of 1 lemon

4 tablespoons gin

600g (1lb 5oz) piece of good-quality skin-on salmon fillet (from the thicker, wider part of the fish, if possible)

blinis, refreshed in a frying pan, to serve

For the quick-pickled cucumber

1 small cucumber, thinly sliced

100ml (3½fl oz) white wine vinegar

2 tablespoons sugar

1 tablespoon salt

For the horseradish crème fraîche

200g (7oz) crème fraîche

1 teaspoon hot horseradish sauce

OTHER WINES

Dry French rosés, such as those from the Languedoc or the Rhône. Pink Champagne or similar sparkling wine is a great fit for an elevated moment.

This is my dad's festive recipe, perfected over the years – the delicate flavours and freshness in the rosé and the cured salmon offer a welcome break from richer dishes. But it's also a great year-round recipe that looks fab. It's perfect for a nibble or a starter, and just needs a little forward planning. Elegant, fresh rosés – especially from Provence – have gentle fruit notes (stone fruit, red berries, sometimes a hint of melon), bright acidity, floral lift and a subtle saline edge. They bring freshness to the richness and umami of the salmon, mirror the beetroot's earthy sweetness, and balance the citrus zest and botanical notes in the gin cure. The textures align beautifully too: soft, silky salmon with a glass of cool, crisp rosé.

In a food processor, blitz the beetroot, sea salt, sugar, pepper, lemon zest and gin to a coarse paste. Alternatively, grate the beetroot and mix with the other ingredients. Lay a large sheet of clingfilm on the work surface and place the salmon on top, skin side down. Press the cure evenly over the salmon and wrap tightly in the clingfilm. Place in a shallow dish and leave to cure in the fridge for 36–48 hours.

Remove the cure and gently wash the salmon under a cold tap. Pat dry and place on a board, flesh side up. Using a sharp knife, slice the salmon at an angle into 5mm (½ inch) thick slices, gliding over the skin so the flesh is removed, leaving the skin intact.

Combine the cucumber ingredients in a dish, set aside for 1 hour (or longer) to pickle, then drain.

Mix together the crème fraîche and horseradish and serve with the salmon and cucumber.

Beaujolais with cheese and meat board

SERVES 6

300g (10½oz) selection of cheese, such as Brillat-savarin, Comté, Brie, goats' cheese crottin

100g (3½oz) duck rillettes

100g (3½oz) French torchon ham

100g (3½oz) air-dried ham

100g (3½oz) salami

To serve

cornichons

pickled onions

crusty baguette

salted butter

If you think red wines are a no-go for apéro hour, let me show you how it can be done. Beaujolais is a brilliant option – all juicy red fruit, light tannins and bright acidity. Some styles are more structured and savoury, but look for bottles labelled 'Beaujolais', 'Beaujolais-Villages', or the *Crus* (specific villages) such as Brouilly or Fleurie (lighter) or Morgon (more structured). These are soft, perfumed reds that can be served lightly chilled to bring out their fruit and freshness. I like to pair them with a casual cheese and meat board. The wine's acidity cuts through creamy cheeses and fatty charcuterie, while the salt brings out the juicy fruit of the wine, and the gentle tannins work well for an early evening tipple.

Arrange the cheeses and sliced meats on a board with cornichons and pickled onions for crunch and acidity. Serve with baguette slices and butter.

OTHER WINES

Fruity and low-tannin reds, such as Pinot Noir, Cinsault, Frappato and Valpolicella Classico from cool climates and young in age. White wines with texture and body, such as oaked Chardonnay and Chenin Blanc. Rich-quality traditional-method sparkling wines, particularly Blanc de Noirs styles.

FISH & SEAFOOD

Chablis with scallops and samphire

SERVES 4 AS A STARTER

12 scallops on the half shell, roe removed

100g (3½oz) unsalted butter

100g (3½oz) samphire

zest and juice of ½ lemon

coarse sea salt and pepper

There are so many things I love about this pairing – the buttery, plump texture of scallops cut through by the brisk acidity of Chablis, the lemon zest and salty bite of samphire recalling the wine's citrus and marine character, and the oyster-shell edge that's so typical of this region. There's beautiful flavour synergy and balance here – a little fat, lots of umami, salt and acid all working in union through just a handful of ingredients. Most Chablis is unoaked, or only subtly oaked, which allows the purity and mineral clarity of the wine to shine – ideal with simple seafood dishes like this. When choosing a bottle, avoid the leaner styles of Petit Chablis and look instead for Chablis or Chablis *Premier Cru* (or *Grand Cru* if you're splashing out) for more depth and texture to match the buttery richness of the scallops.

Preheat the grill to medium-high.

Lightly season the scallops and top each with a knob of butter, reserving one-quarter of the butter for the samphire. Grill the scallops for 3–6 minutes, until just cooked and springy to the touch. Alternatively, cook them on a hot barbecue.

Meanwhile, in a small pan over medium heat, melt the remaining butter and sauté the samphire for 2–3 minutes. Turn off the heat and add the lemon juice. Divide the samphire between the scallop shells and top with the lemon zest.

OTHER WINES

Cool-climate unoaked or lightly oaked Chardonnay from England or similar Chardonnays. Crisp, citrus-driven and textured white wines, such as Soave Classico, Albariño or Assyrtiko. Traditional-method sparkling wines, particularly Blanc de Blancs styles.

Albariño with clams in white wine

SERVES 4 AS A STARTER, 2 AS A MAIN

800g–1kg (1lb 12oz–2lb 4oz) live clams, scrubbed

2 tablespoons olive oil, plus extra for drizzling

1 large shallot, finely diced

2 garlic cloves, minced

150ml (5fl oz) white wine

2 tablespoons chopped flat leaf parsley

crusty bread, to serve

The wild, rugged coast of Rías Baixas is the home of Albariño, a fresh, citrusy, saline white that speaks of its Atlantic roots. It's also where I first fell for this incredibly simple but irresistible pairing of local clams cooked with garlic, parsley and white wine – shared with a group of lovely wine women on a trip that still makes me smile. It's a dish that mirrors the wine's clean, ocean energy. The umami richness of the clams is lifted by Albariño's bright acidity, while the citrus and herb notes in the sauce bring out the wine's zesty edge. It really is that simple – but it's a pairing I dream about, ideally with the sea breeze on my face and a glass in hand.

Soak the clams in a bowl of salted water for 1 hour, agitating them every 10 minutes and changing the water until all the grit is removed and the water is clear. Drain the clams and discard any with broken shells.

Heat the olive oil in a large pan on a medium heat. Cook the shallot until translucent, then add the garlic and cook for 1 minute more. Add the clams and the white wine and cover with a lid. Cook for around 5 minutes, tossing the pan intermittently to circulate the juices and heat, until the shells have opened. Discard any clams that haven't opened, then stir through the parsley, drizzle with a little extra oil and serve immediately.

OTHER WINES

Crisp, saline white wines, such as Muscadet, Picpoul de Pinet (France) or Vermentino from Italy. Unoaked Chardonnay, such as Chablis.

Muscadet with dressed crab, a pint of prawns and chips

SERVES 2 AS A MAIN

oven chips

2 dressed crabs

2 pints of shell-on cooked prawns (shrimp)

Baby Gem lettuce

lemon wedges

mayonnaise

Here's a pairing that requires zero skill in the kitchen, but looks the part and delivers on flavour and freshness. Muscadet is a coastal white from the Loire, made from the grape Melon de Bourgogne, and it brings a real sea-spray feel to the glass – all bright citrus, briny freshness and a lean, clean finish. It's just right with raw or cold shellfish served with lemon. The wine's refreshing acidity balances the salt, sweetness and soft umami of the shellfish, and gives a lively, cleansing bite. And who doesn't love a hot, crunchy chip alongside a crisp white wine? For Muscadet styles with a bit of body and oomph, look for 'sur lie' on the label – it means the wine has spent time resting on its lees (the post-fermentation yeast), adding a bit more texture.

Cook the oven chips according to the packet instructions and serve with the crabs, prawns, lettuce, lemon wedges and mayonnaise.

OTHER WINES

Crisp, saline white wines, such as Albariño or Picpoul de Pinet, or Italian Verdicchio. Unoaked Chardonnay, such as Chablis.

Picpoul de Pinet with grilled garlic mussels

SERVES 4 AS A STARTER, 2 AS A MAIN

1kg (2lb 4oz) live mussels, scrubbed

50g (1¾oz) butter, softened

2 tablespoons olive oil

3 garlic cloves, minced

zest of ½ lemon

2 tablespoons finely chopped flat leaf parsley

85g (3oz) panko breadcrumbs

coarse sea salt and pepper

To serve

lemon wedges

crusty baguette

Right in the south of the Languedoc sits the Étang de Thau, a saltwater lagoon that produces thousands of tonnes of oysters and mussels each year. And just a few metres back from the shore, you'll find vineyards planted with Picpoul (or Piquepoul), the zingy white that delivers Mediterranean sunshine and salty air. Naturally, the wine and local shellfish pair perfectly – trust me, I've sat by the lagoon indulging in both. This really is a great example of terroir matching. The name 'Picpoul' comes from the French for 'lip-stinger', a nod to its bracingly fresh acidity. And while it's classic with raw oysters and simply cooked mussels, I love it with grilled garlicky mussels – full of flavour, with a smoky edge and all that umami richness and salt. Picpoul's citrus snap and bright acidity cut straight through, lifting the dish and keeping it lively. It's relaxed, full of flavour, and a great way to kick off a dinner.

Discard any mussels with broken shells, then place in a large pan with a splash of water over a high heat and cook for 3–4 minutes, or until the shells have opened. Discard any mussels that haven't opened, then remove one of the shells from each mussel and place the half-shelled mussels on a baking tray, flesh side up.

Preheat the grill to high.

Combine the butter, olive oil, garlic, lemon zest, parsley and panko breadcrumbs in a small bowl and season well. Spoon a little of the mixture onto each mussel and cook under the grill for 2–3 minutes, until golden. Serve immediately, with lemon wedges for squeezing over the mussels and crusty baguette.

OTHER WINES

Crisp, saline white wines, such as Albariño, Muscadet or Assyrtiko.

Godello with fideuà

SERVES 6–8 AS A MAIN

2 tablespoons olive oil

500g (1lb 2oz) fideos or broken vermicelli

1 large tomato, finely diced

1 large onion, finely diced

1 teaspoon smoked paprika

4 garlic cloves, minced

700ml (1¼ pints) good-quality seafood stock

300ml (10fl oz) hot water

a few saffron strands (optional)

500g (1lb 2oz) raw peeled prawns (shrimp)

200g (7oz) prepared squid, diced

250g (9oz) monkfish, cut into chunks

chopped flat leaf parsley, to garnish

To serve

aioli

lemon wedges

Ever since discovering this variation on the Spanish classic paella – made with short noodles instead of rice – fideuà has been a dish I've frequently dreamed of with a glass of glorious Godello, in reach of the sea. But with the reality of city life and not as much time to cook as I'd like, I've developed a shortcut home version, using quality pre-made fish stock to drastically reduce the prep. The result still feels like a showstopper, served in a wide, shallow pan for everyone to dive in. With all the mellow, savoury depth from the stock and shellfish, you could reach for a fresh Albariño for contrast, but I prefer Godello, leaning into something a bit plusher and layered. It has a weightier texture, often with ripe citrus, peach and mineral notes – Spain's answer to white Burgundy. It has enough depth to stand up to the flavours, a rounded texture to complement the richness, and just the right acidity to keep everything feeling bright.

Heat the olive oil in a 46cm (18 inch) paella pan over a medium heat, add the fideos and toast until lightly golden. Remove from the pan and set aside. Add the tomato and onion to the pan and cook gently for a few minutes, until the onion is translucent, then add the paprika and garlic.

On a low heat, return the fideos to the pan, slowly add the stock, hot water and saffron, if using, and bring to a gentle bubble for 5 minutes, making sure not to stir so that the pasta forms a crispy bottom (known as the *socarrat*).

Reduce the heat, nestle the seafood among the noodles and cook for 6–8 minutes, until the stock has been absorbed and the seafood is cooked through. Sprinkle with parsley and serve immediately, with big dollops of aioli and lemon wedges.

OTHER WINES

Textured styles of white, such as oaked Chardonnay or white Rioja, or zesty whites, such as Albariño.

Dry Riesling with sea bass crudo

SERVES 4 AS A STARTER

4 small skinless, boneless sea bass fillets

juice of 2 limes

2 tablespoons olive oil

small pinch of golden caster sugar (superfine sugar)

pinch of coarse sea salt

To garnish

1 tablespoon chopped fresh coriander (cilantro)

½ green apple, cut into matchsticks

1 radish, thinly sliced

1 green chilli, thinly sliced

zest of 1 lime

microgreens

Dry Riesling is the wine that got me into wine. It's wildly distinct from most other whites, with vibrant citrus, floral flair and bracing acidity that can hit like a lightning bolt; we fans of this style are aptly called 'acid heads'. From a culinary perspective, there's so much to play with. This quick crudo pairing is all about light, zesty, high-energy flavours. The lime, crisp apple and coriander reflect the citrus and mineral edge of the wine, while the acidity across both dish and glass brings a clean, fresh lift. A pinch of coarse sea salt brightens the flavours and rounds out the texture of the wine. My pick is a dry, racy German Riesling – look to the Mosel and check the label for the word *trocken* (dry), or in most cases, anything above 11.5% ABV is likely to be dry.

Place the sea bass in the freezer for 15 minutes to firm up, then finely slice the fillets against the grain and assemble on a large plate. Drizzle with the lime juice, olive oil, sugar and coarse sea salt and allow to sit for 10–15 minutes to gently cure.

Sprinkle with the coriander, green apple, radish and chilli and finish with the lime zest and microgreens.

OTHER WINES

Dry Riesling from Alsace, Australia (Clare and Eden Valleys) or USA (Finger Lakes). Crisp and zesty white wines, such as Etna Bianco (Sicily), Vermentino, Albariño, and those with a herbaceous edge such as Sauvignon Blanc and Grüner Veltliner.

Off-dry Riesling with spicy prawn noodle salad

SERVES 2 AS A MAIN

100g (3½oz) rice vermicelli

1 tablespoon olive oil, plus extra for drizzling

2 garlic cloves, finely minced

1–2 red bird's eye chillies, finely diced

300g (10½oz) raw peeled prawns (shrimp)

2 small handfuls of mint, torn

2 small handfuls of fresh coriander (cilantro), torn

2 small carrots, julienned

½ cucumber, julienned

5 radishes, finely sliced

1 small mango, peeled and diced

2 tablespoons crushed salted peanuts

1 tablespoon toasted sesame seeds

salt and pepper

lime wedges, to serve

For the dressing

3 tablespoons soy sauce

1 tablespoon sesame oil

1 tablespoon brown sugar or golden caster sugar (superfine sugar)

zest and juice of 1 lime

This hot and fresh salad has been a healthy go-to for me since backpacking through Thailand in the mid-noughties. Back then it was washed down with a Chang beer or a mango lassi – now I love it with a zingy off-dry Riesling. The salad brings vibrant fresh flavours, so there's great flavour synergy with the wine's fruit and floral profile. Off-dry Riesling has just enough sweetness to soften the chilli, with that little bit of sugar teaming nicely with the mango, all tied together with a citrusy lift in the wine that mirrors the dressing. On a German label, an off-dry style usually sits between 8 and 11.5% ABV.

Cook the noodles according to packet instructions, then drain and place in a wide bowl with a drizzle of oil to stop them sticking together.

Heat the olive oil in a frying pan over a medium heat, add the garlic, chilli and prawns and cook until the prawns are just turning pink. Season to taste, then turn off the heat.

Add the herbs and vegetables to the noodles and toss well. Shake the dressing ingredients together in a jar and dress the salad according to taste. Top with the prawns, peanuts and sesame seeds and serve with lime wedges for squeezing over.

OTHER WINES

Off-dry Riesling from Finger Lakes (New York State, USA). Honeyed styles of Chenin, such as Vouvray from the Loire, off-dry styles of Pinot Gris from Alsace, or aromatic Torrontes from Argentina.

Assyrtiko with prawn saganaki

SERVES 4 AS A MAIN

2 tablespoons olive oil

2 small onions, finely diced

3 garlic cloves, minced

1 tablespoon fresh oregano or 1 teaspoon dried

1 tablespoon chopped parsley, plus extra to garnish

1 red chilli, finely chopped

200g (7oz) cherry tomatoes

400g (14oz) can plum tomatoes

100ml (3½fl oz) dry white wine

juice of ½ lemon

400g (14oz) raw peeled king prawns

200g (7oz) feta cheese, crumbled

black pepper

To serve

lemon wedges

crusty bread

green salad dressed with olive oil and lemon juice

A pairing designed to whisk you away to the Greek islands – an enchanting pick for a summer's evening, but the richness of flavour makes it a year-round favourite. The combination of minerality, precision and tension in Greece's flagship white grape, Assyrtiko, has drawn comparisons with fine Chablis. Grown on the islands (with standout examples from Santorini and Crete) as well as the mainland, it's a natural match for seafood, but its structure means it can stand up to bold, savoury flavours too. Here the wine's acidity mirrors the brightness of the tomatoes, while the salt in the feta lifts its fruit profile and adds to its texture.

Heat the olive oil in an ovenproof frying pan over a medium heat, add the onion, and cook until translucent. Add the garlic, oregano, parsley and chilli and stir for 1 minute. Add the cherry tomatoes, plum tomatoes, white wine and lemon juice and bubble for 20 minutes to reduce and thicken.

Meanwhile, preheat the oven to 180°C (160°C fan), 350°F, Gas Mark 4.

Add the prawns to the pan and sprinkle the feta on top. Finish the dish in the oven for 8–10 minutes, until the prawns are cooked through and the feta begins to melt. Serve immediately with ground black pepper and lemon wedges, plus crusty bread and a simply dressed salad on the side.

OTHER WINES

Citrusy, mineral and fresh whites, such as Chablis, Albariño and Etna Bianco. Juicy rosé wines, such as Spanish Garnacha or Greek Agiorgitiko. Very light reds with fruity flavours and high acidity, such as Frappato.

Vinho Verde with fish tacos

SERVES 4

100g (3½oz) plain flour (all-purpose flour)

½ teaspoon paprika

½ teaspoon dried chilli flakes (red pepper flakes)

zest of ½ lime

2 eggs, beaten

150g (5½oz) fine polenta

vegetable oil, for shallow frying

500g (1lb 2oz) skinless, boneless cod fillet, cut into bite-sized pieces

8–12 soft corn tortillas

salt and pepper

Suggestions for toppings

lime wedges

fresh coriander (cilantro)

finely diced green chillies

tomato salsa

pickled red onions

pickled jalapeños

crispy onions

soured cream

smashed avocado

OTHER WINES

Vibrant whites with bright acidity, such as Albariño, Txakoli or Picpoul de Pinet. Aromatic and crisp whites, such as Bacchus or Sauvignon Blanc.

Taco night is a regular in my house – easy, fun and just the excuse to open something punchy and energetic, a wine that tastes a little like a margarita cocktail to get the evening going. Portugal's white Vinho Verde wines – often made from a blend of grapes, such as Loureiro, Arinto and Alvarinho (aka Albariño in Spain) – are just the pairing: crisp and refreshing with citrus, green apple and mineral notes. Traditionally low in alcohol, they're a real crowd-pleaser for informal, help-yourself-style taco nights – bright, fresh and full of personality (though there are more serious, age-worthy styles too). The wine's acidity cuts through the crunch and fat of fried fish, while its citrusy zip delivers brilliantly with toppings such as lime, coriander and green chilli.

Place the flour in a bowl and mix in the paprika, chilli flakes, lime zest, salt and pepper. Place the eggs in a second bowl and the polenta in a third. Dip the fish pieces in the flour to coat, tapping off the excess, then in the eggs, then the polenta. Heat the oil in a deep-sided frying pan until a crumb sizzles. Fry the fish until cooked through and golden on both sides.

Heat the tortillas according to packet instructions, then wrap in foil to keep them warm. Serve the fish and tortillas with a range of toppings in individual bowls.

Oaked Chardonnay with halibut and a lumpfish roe butter sauce

SERVES 2 AS A MAIN

1 shallot, finely diced

¼ glass of white wine

1 tablespoon white wine vinegar

2 halibut fillets, 150–175g (5½–6oz) each

2 tablespoons olive oil

100g (3½oz) cold unsalted butter, cubed

juice of ¼ lemon

½ teaspoon chopped tarragon

1 teaspoon red lumpfish roe

1 teaspoon black lumpfish roe

salt and pepper

To serve

buttered fine green beans

creamy mashed potato

An opulent menu for a candlelit dinner for two. This pairing is all about finesse and velvety textures in both the wine and the dish, with a little pop of salty intrigue from the lumpfish roe. The sauce's buttery richness, citrus lift and saline edge are made for an elegant oaked Chardonnay – ideally from Bourgogne. If the budget allows, look to the elegant wines from villages such as Puligny-Montrachet in the Côte de Beaune, which offer just the right balance of acidity to cut through the sauce, layered citrus and stone fruit, mineral depth and refined toasty oak. These wines brings structure and lift.

Preheat the oven to 200°C (180°C fan), 400°F, Gas Mark 6.

Place the shallot, white wine and vinegar in a small pan on a low heat and reduce by half. Pass through a sieve, discard the shallot and set the liquid aside.

Season the halibut with salt and pepper. Heat the oil in an ovenproof frying pan on a medium-high heat and sear the fish, skin side down, for 2–3 minutes. Transfer it to the oven for another 5 minutes, until cooked through.

Reheat the wine reduction on a very gentle heat, adding the butter one lump at a time and stirring well to emulsify it. Turn off the heat and add the lemon juice, tarragon and red and black lumpfish roe. Spoon the sauce over the fish immediately and serve alongside green beans and mashed potato.

OTHER WINES

Similar refined oaked Chardonnays from cooler regions of California (Sonoma Coast, Santa Barbara), Oregon, Australia (Yarra Valley, Mornington Peninsula), Argentina (Patagonia), New Zealand (Auckland) and South Africa (Hemel-en-Aarde).

Grüner Veltliner with a herby trout salad

SERVES 4 AS A MAIN

100g (3½oz) dried bulgur wheat

4 trout fillets, 150–175g (5½–6oz) each

2 tablespoons olive oil

juice of ½ lemon

150g (5½oz) rocket

2 celery sticks, finely diced

1 fennel bulb, diced, fronds reserved for garnish

2 grapefruits, segmented

½ cucumber, peeled into ribbons

salt and pepper

lemon wedges, to serve

For the vinaigrette

1 teaspoon Dijon mustard

2 tablespoons red wine vinegar

juice of ½ lemon

6 tablespoons olive oil

pinch of salt

½ teaspoon ground white pepper

1 teaspoon finely chopped dill

Fresh acidity, green snap and a whisper of pepper make this wine and recipe pairing a bright, lively match. Grüner Veltliner's fruit, gentle herbaceous notes and touch of spice have great intensity and affinity with the clean, mineral character of trout, juicy grapefruit, and the layers of fennel, dill and peppery vinaigrette in the salad. There's a hint of bitterness from the greens and herbs, which marries well with Grüner's herby character and signature touch of white pepper. The overall effect is crisp, pure and vibrant – a great showcase for Austria's flagship white.

Cook the bulgur wheat according to the packet instructions and allow to cool.

Preheat the oven to 180°C (160°C fan), 350°F, Gas Mark 4.

Place the trout fillets in an oven dish lined with nonstick baking paper and drizzle with the olive oil, lemon juice and a pinch of salt. Bake for 12 minutes for a juicy, just-cooked texture.

Combine all the vinaigrette ingredients in a jam jar and shake to emulsify.

In a shallow serving bowl, combine the bulgur wheat, rocket, celery, fennel, grapefruit and cucumber. Season to taste, drizzle over some of the vinaigrette (there will be some left over) and mix gently with salad servers. Flake the cooked trout on top of the salad, garnish with the reserved fennel fronds and serve with lemon wedges.

OTHER WINES

Herb-friendly, crisp whites, such as English Bacchus, Loire Sauvignon Blanc, Albariño, Vermentino.

Deep-hued rosé with tuna niçoise

SERVES 4 AS A MAIN

4 fresh tuna steaks, about 175g (6oz) each

1 tablespoon grapeseed oil

2 Baby Gem lettuces, leaves separated, or 1 Butterhead lettuce

500g (1lb 2oz) baby new potatoes, boiled and halved

250g (9oz) fine green beans, blanched

200g (7oz) mixed cherry tomatoes, halved

6 eggs, soft-boiled and halved

1 small red onion, finely sliced

150g (5½oz) Kalamata olives or similar

50g (1¾oz) can anchovy fillets, drained

2 tablespoons capers

For the dressing

6 tablespoons olive oil

2 tablespoons red wine vinegar

2 teaspoons Dijon mustard

salt and pepper

For a taste of summer the French way, pair a gastronomic, deeply coloured rosé – such as one from Tavel in the Rhône – with a chic, contemporary take on tuna niçoise. These dry, darker-hued rosés are typically packed with crunchy red berry fruit and plenty of acidity, so they mirror the vibrancy of the salad and match it in flavour intensity. There's a mineral freshness in the wine, which complements the briny, zesty hit of capers, anchovies and olives, their saltiness bringing out the fruit in the wine. Tuna steaks have a meaty richness that stands up beautifully to this bold, structured style of rosé.

Season the tuna steaks with a little salt. Heat the grapeseed oil in a frying pan on a high heat, then flash-fry the steaks for 30–45 seconds per side to form a crust. They should remain pink inside. Remove from the pan and allow to rest for a few minutes before slicing across the grain into strips.

Arrange the lettuce leaves on a large serving plate, then layer the potatoes, green beans, tomatoes and eggs on top. Add the seared tuna, then top with the red onion, olives, anchovies and capers.

Mix the dressing ingredients together and drizzle over the salad.

OTHER WINES

Similar deep-hued rosés from Navarra or Campo de Borja in Spain. Paler, but structured French rosés, such as those from Bandol. Very light reds, for example certain styles of Gamay (Beaujolais).

Provence rosé with spicy salmon skewers

SERVES 2 AS A MAIN

100g (3½oz) full-fat Greek yogurt

1 garlic clove, minced

1 teaspoon smoked paprika

1 teaspoon ground cumin

1 teaspoon sumac

1 teaspoon ground turmeric

1 red chilli, deseeded and finely chopped

zest and juice of 1 lemon

650g (1lb 7oz) skinless salmon fillet, cut into 3–4cm (1¼–1½ inch) cubes

salt and pepper

To serve

flatbreads, flashed under a grill to soften

pomegranate, feta, dill and couscous salad

A pretty pairing that can be rustled up in half an hour, this works particularly well for a light al fresco lunch. It's a brilliant way to show off the versatility of rosé with a little spice. The soft red fruit, dry elegance and refreshing acidity of Provence rosé work beautifully with these lightly aromatic, chilli-marinated salmon skewers. There's a satisfying balance between the warmth of the spice, the char from the grill, and the cool lift of the wine. A pomegranate, feta, dill and couscous salad on the side adds brightness and texture, with the fruit evoking the wine's berry notes, and the feta picking up on its mineral charm.

Soak a few wooden skewers in water for at least 30 minutes to prevent them from burning.

Mix the yogurt, garlic, smoked paprika, cumin, sumac, turmeric, red chilli, lemon juice and zest in a bowl with some seasoning. Add the salmon, toss to coat and leave to marinate in the fridge for 15–60 minutes.

Heat the grill to high. Remove the salmon and place a few cubes on each skewer. Cook under the grill for 8–10 minutes, until a little charred but still tender. Serve with the flatbreads and salad.

OTHER WINES

Similar dry, pale styles of rosé from the Languedoc or Rhône Valley in France. Similar dry styles from regions such as Italy, Spain or England.

Barbera with tomato, bean and squid stew

SERVES 4 AS A STARTER, OR 2 AS A MAIN

1 tablespoon olive oil

1 onion, finely diced

2 garlic cloves, minced

1 dried bay leaf

½ teaspoon dried oregano

400g (14oz) can plum tomatoes

zest and juice of ½ lemon

300g (10½oz) prepared squid, cut into rings and tentacles

400g (14oz) can butter beans (lima beans), rinsed and drained

1 tablespoon chopped flat leaf parsley

salt and pepper

To serve

simply dressed rocket salad

rustic bread, charred

olive oil

This speedy stew is rustic and full of depth, with a velvety, intense tomato base that calls for a lighter, fruit-forward red. My pick for this Italian-influenced recipe is Barbera, from Piedmont in northwest Italy. With its juicy red fruit, relatively low tannins and fresh acidity, it's a great match for the richness and umami in the stew. The acidity cuts through the tomato base, while the fruit contrasts with the seasoning and salt, and there's lovely flavour synergy between the herbs in the dish and those often found in the wine. A bold-flavoured pairing with just the right freshness to keep it balanced.

Heat the oil in a medium pan over a gentle heat and add the onion. Cook until translucent, then add the garlic, bay leaf and oregano and cook for 1 minute more. Add the tomatoes and break up with a wooden spoon. Add the lemon zest, lower the heat and cook to reduce for 10 minutes.

Turn up the heat to medium and add the squid, then continue to simmer for 5 minutes. Add the butter beans and cook for another 3 minutes. Season with salt and pepper to taste, then add the lemon juice and parsley. Serve with a rocket salad and charred bread, drizzled with olive oil.

OTHER WINES

Pinot Nero (the Italian name for Pinot Noir) from Alto Adige.

Côtes du Rhône with cod and tapenade crumb

SERVES 2

100g (3½oz) pitted black olives

2 tablespoons panko breadcrumbs

1 teaspoon dried oregano

zest of ½ lemon

1 tablespoon olive oil, plus extra for greasing

pinch of black pepper

2 skinless cod fillets, about 200g (7oz) each

2 vines of cherry tomatoes

For the potatoes

300g (10½oz) baby new potatoes

1 tablespoon olive oil

small sprig of rosemary

2 garlic cloves, crushed

salt and pepper

OTHER WINES

Rhône-style reds from Santa Barbara (California, USA) or McLaren Vale (Australia). Youthful (Crianza) styles of Rioja, fruity styles of Beaujolais, light styles of Spanish Garnacha, or Cinsault from South Africa or Chile.

A wine trip to the southern Rhône offered a fresh perspective on pairing red wine with fish – here it was embraced, not seen as a faux pas. The key was choosing a youthful, Grenache-dominant style of Côtes du Rhône, with soft red fruit, supple body, and a little spice and dried herb complexity. When paired with fish dishes that carry bold Mediterranean flavours, it worked beautifully. This quick tapenade topping brings those flavours into the kitchen – a herby, salty crust with lovely depth. The sweetness of the roasted tomatoes picks up on the wine's fruit, while the tapenade and olive oil echo its subtle spice and peppery lift. The wine's smooth body supports the flaky cod without overpowering it.

Preheat the oven to 200°C (180°C fan), 400°F, Gas Mark 6.

Place all the ingredients for the potatoes in a bowl and toss to coat. Transfer to a baking tray and roast in the oven for about 25 minutes, depending on size, until crisp on the outside and soft inside.

Meanwhile, pulse the olives, breadcrumbs, oregano, lemon zest, olive oil and black pepper in a food processor to form a coarse tapenade.

Place the cod in a greased ovenproof dish with the vines of cherry tomatoes. Spread a generous layer of tapenade on top of the cod and bake for 10–12 minutes, until the fish just begins to flake.

POULTRY & MEAT

Red Rioja with Mediterranean chicken

SERVES 4

8 skin-on chicken thighs

½ teaspoon smoked paprika

1 small onion, diced

3 garlic cloves, minced

1 tablespoon capers

1 teaspoon thyme leaves

50g (1¾oz) can anchovy fillets, drained and chopped

2 x 400g (14oz) cans plum tomatoes

3 tablespoons pitted black olives

pepper

1 tablespoon chopped flat leaf parsley, to garnish

To serve

green salad

sautéd potatoes

This is just the pairing for an impromptu dinner with friends – everything goes into one pot while you pour a glass, chat and wait for those gorgeous Mediterranean aromas to fill the kitchen. Red Rioja wines (based on the Tempranillo grape) range from fresh and fruity styles to the increasingly complex, oak-aged expressions labelled Crianza, Reserva and Gran Reserva (the last being the longest aged and most complex). For this dish, go for a crowd-pleasing Crianza or Reserva with a little bottle age – expect red and black fruit, savoury tomato and leather notes, Mediterranean herbs and gentle oak spice. Both the wine and the dish bring together rich fruit and earthy, savoury elements deliciously. This mid-weight style has enough acidity and tannic structure to stand up to the fatty roast chicken skin, while still offering the freshness and lift to keep everything in balance.

Preheat the oven to 220°C (200°C fan), 425°F, Gas Mark 7.

Set a wide flameproof casserole dish on the hob over a medium heat. Place half the chicken thighs in the casserole, skin side down, and cook until golden all over to render the fat. Transfer to a plate, then fry the remaining thighs in the same way. Add to the other fried thighs, then rub with smoked paprika and season with pepper. Set aside.

Add the onion to the casserole and cook until golden, before adding the garlic, capers and thyme. Cook for 1–2 minutes, then add the anchovies and tomatoes, breaking up the tomatoes with a wooden spoon. Place the chicken on top, skin side up, and scatter the olives around. Place the dish in the oven and cook uncovered for 20–25 minutes, until the chicken is cooked through, then scatter with chopped parsley to serve.

OTHER WINES

Similar styles of red that balance fruit and savoury notes with good acidity, such as Chianti Classico, Côtes du Rhône or Rhône-style reds from USA or Australia. Robust, deeper dry rosé, such as Spanish styles from Navarra or French styles from Tavel.

Off-dry Riesling with one-pot green curry

SERVES 4 AS A MAIN

8 skin-on boneless chicken thighs

2 tablespoons Thai green curry paste

400ml (14fl oz) can coconut milk

200ml (7fl oz) chicken stock

2 tablespoons fish sauce

2 tablespoons dark brown sugar

zest and juice of 2 limes

200g (7oz) jasmine rice, rinsed

1 ripe mango, diced

2 pak choi, quartered

handful of coriander (cilantro) leaves

1 green chilli, finely diced

salt

lime wedges, to serve

Sweeter styles of Riesling in the off-dry to medium-sweet range are a classic match for fragrant, spicy dishes – and green curry is one of the best examples. Here's a simple one-pot recipe that's ideal for a midweek supper (saving on the washing up) and full of flavour too. In this recipe, the zesty notes in the curry paste – lemongrass, lime leaves – mirror Riesling's zing, while its bright acidity lifts the creamy coconut milk. There's a lovely sweetness across the wine and the mango and palm sugar in the sauce, and the wine's residual sugar softens the impact of the chilli, giving a satisfying balance. A seamless play of bold flavours, sweetness, fat, freshness and heat.

Preheat the oven to 180°C (160°C fan), 350°F, Gas Mark 4.

Set a wide flameproof casserole dish on the hob over a medium heat. Place half the chicken thighs in the pan, skin side down, and cook until golden all over to render the fat. Transfer to a plate, then fry the remaining thighs in the same way. Add to the other fried thighs and set aside.

Add the curry paste to the casserole with the coconut milk, chicken stock, fish sauce, sugar, lime zest and juice and stir until smooth. Add the rice and mango and stir through gently.

Nestle the chicken thighs on the top, skin side up, and season with salt. Bake for 20–25 minutes, then add the pak choi. Return to the oven for a further 10 minutes, until the chicken and rice are cooked through. Scatter with the coriander leaves and green chilli, and serve with lime wedges.

OTHER WINES

Pinot Gris from Alsace with a little sweetness. Off-dry styles of Chenin Blanc, for example from Vouvray in the Loire. Aromatic Torrontes from Chile. Sweeter styles of sparkling wine.

Viognier with chicken and pumpkin pie

SERVES 4 AS A MAIN

1 sheet of ready-rolled puff pastry, cut into 4 equal pieces

1 tablespoon grapeseed oil

2–3 skinless chicken breasts, cut into 3cm (1¼ inch) pieces

1 shallot, finely diced

3 garlic cloves, minced

1 small pumpkin, peeled, deseeded and cubed

200ml (7fl oz) chicken stock

200ml (7fl oz) double cream (heavy cream)

pinch of grated nutmeg

3 tablespoons medium-dry Madeira, such as Verdelho (optional)

1 tablespoon white wine vinegar

1 egg, beaten

4 sage leaves

salt and white pepper

This pairing is all about delivering something cosy, comforting and creamy, lifted by subtle aromatics in both the wine and the dish. The best Viogniers offer textural weight, ripe stone fruit, and nuances of florals, spice and white pepper. This chicken and pumpkin pie leans into Viognier's richness, with the weight of the creamy sauce, and draws out its fragrance with nutmeg and white pepper. There's a lovely chime between the stone fruit character in the wine and the gentle sweetness of the pumpkin. Viognier's home is the Rhône Valley, with benchmark examples from the tiny, prestigious Condrieu appellation. For similar premium styles, try Paso Robles (California) or Eden Valley (Australia).

Preheat the oven to 200°C (180°C fan), 400°F, Gas Mark 6, and take the puff pastry out of the fridge 20 minutes before using, so it's easier to unroll.

Heat the oil in a frying pan on a high heat and brown the chicken pieces all over, then remove from the pan and set aside.

Reduce the heat and sauté the shallot in the pan until translucent. Add the garlic and pumpkin and cook, stirring, for a few minutes. Return the chicken to the pan with the stock, cream, nutmeg and Madeira, if using. Season with salt and white pepper and cook for a few minutes to reduce and thicken. Turn off the heat and add the white wine vinegar.

Divide the mixture between 4 individual pie dishes and top with the puff pastry, trimming it to fit. Slit a steam hole in the top of each pie, brush the pastry with beaten egg and garnish with a sage leaf. Bake for 20 minutes, until puffed and golden.

OTHER WINES

Similarly rich Marsanne-Roussanne blends from the Rhône Valley, USA and Australia. Richer styles of Chenin Blanc from the Loire or South Africa. Fiano from Italy.

Chenin Blanc with chicken, tarragon and pears

SERVES 4 AS A MAIN

zest of ½ orange

2 tablespoons olive oil

2 teaspoons coarse salt

½ teaspoon pepper, plus extra to serve

1 small chicken, spatchcocked

2 pears, quartered

4 banana shallots, peeled and halved

1 small glass of white wine

1 tablespoon honey

1 tablespoon butter

1 tablespoon chopped tarragon

To serve

creamy mashed potato

wilted greens

Richer styles of Chenin Blanc are a joy to pair with chicken – they bring weighted texture, expressive orchard fruit and a mineral bite to cut through the richness. Chenin's home is the Loire Valley, but my heart lies with old-vine examples from South Africa, especially the concentrated, layered styles from Swartland. In this dish, the warmth and sweetness of orange zest, pears and honey mirror the ripe, honeyed notes in the wine, while tarragon adds a gentle herbal lift to complement the wine's floral, mineral character. Harmonious and heartening – a pairing for the soul and for hungry guests.

Preheat the oven to 200°C (180°C fan), 400°F, Gas Mark 6.

In a small bowl, combine the orange zest, olive oil, salt and pepper. Place the chicken in a roasting dish, skin side up, and rub the mixture over it. Nestle the pears and shallots in the dish around the chicken, then add the wine. Roast for 30 minutes.

Meanwhile, melt the honey and butter in a small pan on a low heat. Brush over the chicken, pears and shallots, then return to the oven for a further 10 minutes, until the chicken is cooked through and golden. Cover with foil and rest for 20 minutes, then scatter with the tarragon and extra pepper. Serve with mash and greens.

OTHER WINES

Similarly rich whites, oaked styles of Chardonnay from Burgundy and other similar styles. Rhône whites, oaked styles of white Bordeaux (typically a blend of Sauvignon Blanc and Semillon). Rich styles of Pinot Gris (Alsace, Oregon, New Zealand).

Pinot Noir with confit duck, blood orange and sweet potato

SERVES 4 AS A MAIN

4 confit duck legs, fat scraped off

2 large sweet potatoes, peeled and chopped

olive oil

handful of hazelnuts

1 head of radicchio, leaves separated

2 blood oranges, zested, peeled and cut into segments

salt and pepper

For the jus

juice of 2 blood oranges

3 tablespoons red wine vinegar

2 teaspoons honey

100ml (3½fl oz) chicken or vegetable stock

1 tablespoon butter

OTHER WINES

Savoury styles of Pinot Noir from Sonoma Coast or Santa Barbara (California), Mornington Peninsula or Yarra Valley (Australia), Martinborough or Central Otago (New Zealand). German Spätburgunder (the German name for Pinot Noir) or Beaujolais Cru wines, such as those from Morgon.

A stylish dish with visual flair that looks far more technical than it is – especially when using pre-cooked confit legs. It makes a divine match for Bourgogne Pinot Noir, or similar styles, such as those from Oregon. Known for its elegance, red fruit, umami and earthy autumnal notes, the wine's bright acidity cuts through the richness of the duck. Its savoury character pairs beautifully with the toasted warmth of hazelnuts and gamey meat, and there's a sophisticated harmony in the restrained red fruit and the lift of blood orange, which also softens the gentle bitterness of the radicchio.

Heat the confit duck legs according to packet instructions, until crispy.

Cook the sweet potatoes in boiling salted water until tender, then mash with a little olive oil and season to taste.

Heat a teaspoon of olive oil in a frying pan over a medium heat, add the hazelnuts and toast until golden. Remove from the pan and set aside to cool slightly, then roughly chop. In the same pan, gently wilt the radicchio leaves in the hazelnut oil until softened.

For the jus, heat the orange juice, vinegar, honey and stock in a small saucepan and simmer for 5–7 minutes, until slightly reduced. Remove from the heat and whisk in the butter until glossy. Season to taste.

Divide the sweet potato mash between 4 plates, top with the duck legs, scatter with the radicchio, hazelnuts, orange segments and zest, then drizzle with the jus to serve.

Garnacha with warm duck salad

SERVES 4 AS A MAIN

4 skin-on duck breasts

3 teaspoons Chinese five spice powder

300g (10½oz) baby heritage carrots, peeled

100ml (3½fl oz) water

1 chicory (endive) heart, leaves separated

150g (5½oz) kale, stalks discarded, leaves finely shredded

handful of radishes, sliced

handful of pomegranate seeds

salt and pepper

For the vinaigrette

4 tablespoons olive oil

1 tablespoon red wine vinegar

1 tablespoon orange juice

1 tablespoon lemon juice

1 tablespoon pomegranate molasses

OTHER WINES

Fruit-forward styles of Grenache from California and Australia. Fruit-forward, bolder styles of Pinot Noir from New Zealand or California. Fruity and spiced medium-bodied reds, such as Chianti Classico and Crianza, and Reserva styles of Rioja.

My pick with this attractive duck salad is a lighter style of Garnacha (the Spanish name for Grenache), typically produced in high-altitude Spanish vineyards – from affordable, juicy styles from Campo de Borja to premium, elegant examples from the Gredos Mountains near Madrid. These reds resemble Pinot Noir's ethereal, silky texture and vibrant red fruit with a gentle hint of spice, but offer a bit more cosy warmth – just right with this dish. The charm here is the resonance of the salad's ingredients with Garnacha's profile: pomegranate mirrors the wine's bright fruit, subtle five spice picks up its fragrance, the sweet citrus dressing reflects Garnacha's fruit-forward softness, and the duck's richness finds balance in the wine's mid-weight structure and fresh acidity.

Using a sharp knife, score the skin of the duck breasts, then rub the meat with the five spice powder. Sprinkle some salt in a frying pan on a gentle heat and add the duck, skin side down, to start rendering the fat. Cook for about 10–12 minutes in total, turning when the skin is deep golden, until cooked to your liking – the duck should feel springy to the touch. Remove from the pan and rest under foil for 15 minutes.

Meanwhile, add the carrots and measured water to the pan on a medium heat and cook until tender. Turn off the heat and toss through the chicory and kale to wilt, season to taste, then arrange the warmed vegetables on a large plate. Slice the duck breasts and place on top, then scatter with the radishes and pomegranate. Mix the ingredients for the vinaigrette and dress the salad.

Sangiovese with duck ragu and pappardelle

SERVES 4 AS A MAIN

4 skin-on duck legs

2 onions, finely diced

4 garlic cloves, minced

2 bay leaves

1 tablespoon chopped thyme

2 x 400g (14oz) cans chopped tomatoes

1 teaspoon balsamic vinegar

1 large glass of fruity red wine

500g (1lb 2oz) fresh pappardelle

salt

For the topping

handful of panko breadcrumbs, toasted in a pan with a little butter

1 tablespoon chopped parsley

3 tablespoons grated Parmesan cheese

Picture this: a balmy evening in the Tuscan hills, the sun low and warm, bathing everything in a terracotta glow. Cypress trees wind gracefully across rolling hills peppered with olive groves, and you're ready for dinner, craving something comforting and delicious – something that tastes like the place. So let's tuck into a duck ragu and a beautiful bottle of Sangiovese (key regions include Chianti Classico and Brunello di Montalcino in Tuscany, Emilia-Romagna and Umbria). There's harmony between the ragu's rich, savoury duck and tomato flavours, and Sangiovese's own cherry, tomato leaf and herb notes. Its assertive acidity lifts the richness, while the structured tannins bring pleasant grip. A pairing that speaks to Tuscany's rustic soul – guaranteed to warm hearts.

Preheat the oven to 180°C (160°C fan), 350°F, Gas Mark 4.

Place the duck legs in a flameproof casserole dish and season generously with salt. Cover with a lid. Slow-cook in the oven for 1½ hours, then remove the duck from the casserole, tease the meat off the bones (keeping the skin on for flavour) and pull it apart into large chunks. Set aside.

Add the onions to the casserole dish and sweat it over a medium heat in the duck fat and juices. Once translucent, add the garlic, bay leaves and thyme. After a minute, add the tomatoes, balsamic vinegar and red wine. Simmer for 15 minutes, until reduced and saucy, then turn off the heat and add the duck meat.

Combine the topping ingredients in a small bowl. Just before serving, cook the pappardelle and gently stir it into the ragu, adding a spoonful of reserved pasta water if needed. Sprinkle with the crunchy topping and serve immediately.

OTHER WINES

Savoury reds with high acidity, such as Italian Nebbiolo (Barolo), Barbera and Montepulciano d'Abruzzo, or Rhône Syrah.

Cabernet Franc with pork and Padrón pepper kebabs

SERVES 4 AS A MAIN

12 Padrón peppers, or squares of green bell pepper

600g (1lb 5oz) pork shoulder steak or fillet, cut into 5cm (2 inch) strips

1 teaspoon ground green peppercorns

¼ teaspoon chilli flakes (red pepper flakes)

½ teaspoon smoked paprika

2 teaspoons flaky sea salt

zest and juice of 1 lemon

2 tablespoons olive oil

2 garlic cloves, minced

1 tablespoon finely chopped rosemary

To serve

jacket potatoes with salted butter

watercress and walnut salad, dressed in olive oil and lemon juice

aioli

Here's a pairing to make the often-overlooked Cabernet Franc stick in your repertoire. The Loire is home to this variety, where you'll find both juicy, fruit-driven styles and more complex, age-worthy expressions – with top examples from Saumur-Champigny, Bourgueil and Chinon, or head to the Finger Lakes (New York) for similar styles. Cabernet Franc is a natural with this peppery pork dish: its herbal edge matches the seasoning, while its classic notes of black pepper and gentle smokiness mirror the charred meat. The crunchy red and black fruit gives a lovely lift and contrast to the pork, while the wine's fresh acidity cuts through the fattiness. With its medium weight and balance, Cabernet Franc makes an effortless match for this simple but flavour-packed dish.

Soak a few wooden skewers in water to prevent them burning.

Place the peppers and pork in a large bowl, add the ground green pepper, chilli flakes, paprika, salt, lemon zest and juice, olive oil, garlic and rosemary and toss to coat well. Cover and refrigerate for at least 1 hour.

Light a barbecue or heat a grill until very hot. Skewer the pork and peppers, alternating the components. Cook on the barbecue or under a hot grill until just cooked through with a little smoky charring, about 8–10 minutes. Rest the meat for a few minutes, then serve with buttered jacket potatoes, a lightly dressed green salad and aioli.

OTHER WINES

Crunchy reds with a herbal undertone, such as Spanish Mencía, Rhône Syrah, Chilean Carménère.

Chenin Blanc with honey and miso pork belly

SERVES 4

1kg (2lb 4oz) piece of boneless pork belly

3 tablespoons miso paste

2 thumb-sized pieces of fresh root ginger, peeled and grated

1 tablespoon dark brown sugar

½ teaspoon coarse salt

1 teaspoon table salt

125ml (4fl oz) inexpensive white wine

1 tablespoon honey

50ml (1¾fl oz) boiling water

To serve

steamed jasmine rice

mangetout stir-fried with garlic

If this pairing were a colour, it would be gold. Chenin Blanc, with its depth of honeyed orchard fruit, is a knockout match for the sweet, tender pork belly and its golden, crunchy crackling. It's a sumptuous combination, fitting for a feast. There's a tasty alignment in the slightly earthy – almost woolly – nuance Chenin often carries, which picks up on the umami-forward richness of the miso and pork fat. The salt in the dish sharpens the wine's fruit profile, while Chenin's acidity brings lift and balance. Look to an old-vine South African style (Swartland or Stellenbosch) or concentrated, bottle-aged Loire examples, such as those from Vouvray.

Preheat the oven to 180°C (160°C fan), 350°F, Gas Mark 4.

Begin by patting the pork belly dry, then score the skin with a sharp knife in a criss-cross pattern, at 2.5cm (1 inch) intervals.

In a snug roasting tin, mix the miso, ginger, sugar and coarse salt. Rub the mixture all over the pork flesh, avoiding the skin, and place the joint skin side up in the tin. Rub the skin with the table salt and carefully pour the white wine into the bottom of the tin, avoiding contact with the skin. Roast for 1½ hours.

Increase the oven temperature to 220°C (200°C fan), 425°F, Gas Mark 7, and transfer the pork to a baking tray (reserving the juices in the tin). Roast for a further 20 minutes to crackle the skin. Brush off the excess salt, and rest, uncovered, for 20 minutes before slicing.

Drain and discard the excess fat from the juices in the tin, then add the honey and boiling water to make a sauce. Serve the pork with the rice, mangetout and sauce.

OTHER WINES

Rich styles of white wine, with or without oak, such as oaked Chardonnay or Rhône-style whites. Rich styles of Champagne, particularly Blanc de Noirs styles.

Sparkling rosé with beef carpaccio, truffle mayo and pickled mushrooms

SERVES 4 AS A STARTER

200g (7oz) centre-cut fillet of beef

salt and pepper

micro herbs, to serve

For the pickled mushrooms

100g (3½oz) enoki or shiitake mushrooms

100ml (3½fl oz) white wine vinegar

100ml (3½fl oz) water

1 teaspoon coarse sea salt, plus extra to serve

1 teaspoon granulated sugar

For the truffle mayo

2 tablespoons olive oil, plus extra for drizzling

2 tablespoons mayonnaise

1 teaspoon chopped truffle from a jar, or truffle oil

OTHER WINES

High-quality traditional-method rosé sparkling wines. Light, low-tannin, red fruit and earthy reds, such as some styles of Pinot Noir and Beaujolais.

This pairing is inspired by one of my favourite London restaurants – Trinity – and their signature beef tartare with smoked bone marrow, mushrooms and oscietra caviar, which I once had served alongside a glass of rosé Champagne. I was hooked. This at-home version is a nod to that brilliant balance of indulgence and delicacy. The umami-rich beef, earthy truffle and creamy mayo are offset by the brightness of pickled mushrooms, while a glass of rosé sparkling wine weaves it all together – the berry fruit adding contrast to the savoury depth, the mousse and fresh acidity cutting through the richness, and subtle pastry notes teasing out the dish's rich feel with lightness and finesse.

Roll the beef fillet in salt and pepper, then wrap tightly in clingfilm and freeze for 30 minutes to firm up.

Meanwhile, dice the mushrooms into pieces the size of a sweetcorn kernel. Bring the vinegar, water, coarse salt and sugar to a simmer in a small saucepan, then remove from the heat and add the mushrooms. Leave to pickle for 15 minutes, then drain.

Unwrap the beef and, using an extremely sharp knife, slice as thinly as possible. Place the slices between 2 sheets of nonstick baking paper and gently roll with a rolling pin until paper thin.

For the truffle mayo, combine the olive oil, mayonnaise and chopped truffle.

To serve, carefully peel the beef from the paper and arrange on plates in a single layer. Garnish with small drops of truffle mayo, the pickled mushrooms, micro herbs, a pinch of sea salt and a drizzle of olive oil.

Cabernet Sauvignon with steak, red wine butter and marrow

SERVES 2–4 AS A MAIN

1kg (2lb 4oz) côte de boeuf

1 garlic bulb, split horizontally

2 sprigs of rosemary

knob of unsalted butter

2 marrow bones, cut lengthways

For the red wine butter

5 tablespoons fruity red wine

1 banana shallot, finely diced

1 tablespoon aged balsamic vinegar

100g (3½oz) salted butter, softened

coarse sea salt and pepper

To serve

simply dressed salad leaves

French fries

OTHER WINES

Cabernet-based wines from other US regions, such as Washington State, South Africa (Stellenbosch) and Australia (Margaret River or Coonawarra). Other structured, bold reds with good acidity, such as Rioja *Reserva/ Gran Reserva*, Malbec, Chianti and super Tuscan wines, Aglianico, Nebbiolo and Syrah.

The classic combination of Cabernet Sauvignon and steak is hard to beat. There's harmony in the bold flavour intensity – blackcurrant, cedar and green bell pepper in the wine; deep, meaty richness in the beef; and generous textural weight in both. Cabernet's signature high acidity gives lift, keeping the pairing from feeling heavy, while its powerful tannins meet the fat in cuts such as sirloin or rib-eye, softening their feel and adding a plush sensation. I love adding grilled bone marrow whenever I serve steak – its smoky, umami depth mirrors the savoury notes Cabernet develops with age: leather, tobacco, forest floor. Left Bank Bordeaux remains the benchmark for these structured, Cabernet-based reds, with Napa Valley typically offering a bolder, riper expression.

For the red wine butter, simmer the wine, shallot and vinegar in a small pan over a low heat until reduced to a quarter of its volume. Allow to cool, then mix with the softened butter and season well. Form into a cylinder shape, wrap in nonstick baking paper and chill so it's easy to slice.

Remove the steak from the fridge 45 minutes before cooking. Heat a frying pan over a high heat, then season the steak with salt and sear the fat edge until golden and slightly rendered. Next colour each side of the steak on a high heat, before turning down the temperature and adding the garlic, rosemary and unsalted butter. Baste as the steak cooks to your liking, medium-rare here.

While the steak rests for 20 minutes, preheat the grill to high and season the marrow bones. Cook cut sides up for 15 minutes, until bubbling.

To serve, slice the steak and top with slices of the red wine butter. Serve with the marrow, salad and fries.

Syrah with smoky short rib

SERVES 4 AS A MAIN

1.5kg (3lb 5oz) short ribs

200g (7oz) diced pancetta

300g (10½oz) button mushrooms, halved

2 celery sticks, diced

1 carrot, diced

2 onions, diced

8 garlic cloves, sliced

1 bouquet garni (bay, thyme, rosemary, parsley)

1 bottle of inexpensive red wine

2 tablespoons tomato purée (tomato paste)

2 tablespoons smoked harissa paste

400g (14oz) can plum tomatoes

1 litre (1¼ pints) beef stock

To serve

creamy polenta

honey-roasted Chantenay carrots

As I climbed the steep hill of Hermitage, with the fierce Mistral wind whipping against my skin, I looked down at the Syrah vines clinging defiantly to the slopes, thriving in these exposed, unforgiving conditions. That's the essence of Northern Rhône Syrah: confident and a little wild, as if the wine is born out of struggle. It's that untamed richness that makes it such a natural partner for short ribs. There's umami depth from the smoky sauce of the meat and Syrah's savoury edge; the fat is met by Syrah's firm but refined tannins. Spice, structure and soul – a brooding match for a wintry evening.

Heat a large, heavy-based saucepan over a high heat and sear the short ribs until golden all over and some fat has rendered. Remove the ribs from the pan and set aside, then add the pancetta to the pan with the mushrooms, celery, carrot, onions and garlic. Reduce to a medium heat and cook for 10 minutes, until softened and brown.

Add the bouquet garni, wine, tomato purée, harissa and tomatoes. Return the ribs to the pan, bone side up. Add half the beef stock, cover with a tight lid and simmer for 2–2½ hours, topping up with more stock as necessary.

When the meat begins to pull away from the bones, but before it's tender, remove the lid and cook for a further 30 minutes, reducing the sauce while keeping the meat submerged. Remove the ribs and reduce the sauce a final time, until it's thick and glossy. Place the meat back in the sauce and serve with creamy polenta and carrots.

OTHER WINES

Rhône-style Syrah from Walla Walla or Columbia Valley (Washington State, USA), cool-climate Yarra Valley in Australia, or Hawke's Bay, New Zealand. Other smoky or savoury reds, such as Aglianico, Cabernet Sauvignon or South African Pinotage.

Malbec with smash burger and plum ketchup

SERVES 6

600g (1 lb 5oz) minced beef (20% fat)

2 teaspoons salt

½ teaspoon black pepper

sunflower oil

For the plum ketchup

300g (10½oz) ripe plums, stoned and chopped

45g (1¾oz) dark brown sugar

100ml (3½fl oz) red wine vinegar

½ teaspoon ground allspice

1 tablespoon cornflour (cornstarch), mixed with a dash of water (optional)

To serve

burger buns

red cabbage and herb slaw

French fries

OTHER WINES

Smoky reds with dark fruit undertones, such as Cabernet Sauvignon (and Bordeaux blends), Syrah or Chilean Carménère. Quality Zinfandel, for example from Sonoma Coast or Paso Robles (California, USA), or bold and juicy Puglian Primitivo (as Zinfandel is known in Italy).

After finishing law school in 2011, I fled to Argentina for some much-needed freedom, and those five days in Mendoza – vineyard-hopping with a gaggle of law girls – were a dreamy blur of Malbec, barbecue meat and sunshine. This recipe is a playful nod to that trip, tied together by a plum ketchup that leans into the grape's signature purple fruit. Malbec's bold but smooth tannins cut through the fatty richness of the burger, while its dark fruit and smoky edge chime with the charred meat. Quality Argentine Malbec – often grown at altitude – retains great acidity, which brings freshness and lift to the whole pairing.

For the ketchup, place all the ingredients, except the cornflour, in a heavy-based saucepan and simmer for 45 minutes, stirring as it reduces to prevent it catching. When it's thickened, remove from the heat and leave to cool slightly, then blend to a smooth consistency. Add the cornflour to thicken if required.

Season the beef mince with the salt and pepper and divide into 6 loose balls. Heat a large frying pan on a medium-high heat until hot. Add a little sunflower oil and place 2 or 3 balls of meat in the pan. As they begin to cook, gently smash with a wooden spoon or spatula until the burgers are approximately 1cm (½ inch) thick. Cook for 2 minutes, until browned and crisped, then flip. Cook for a further 2 minutes, until cooked through. Cook the remaining burgers in the same way, then serve immediately with buns, slaw, fries and the ketchup.

Xinomavro with harissa lamb cutlets and pistachio

SERVES 4 AS A MAIN

6 tablespoons full-fat Greek yogurt

1 tablespoon rose harissa, preferably smoked

2 garlic cloves, minced

zest of ½ lemon

1 teaspoon salt

1 tablespoon olive oil

12 French-trimmed lamb cutlets

100g (3½oz) pistachios, very finely ground

To serve

warm flatbreads

tzatziki

pea, mint, radish and pomegranate salad

This alluring Greek red comes alive with the fragrant, meaty and nutty flavours in this lamb dish. Xinomavro, a native Greek variety, is often likened to Nebbiolo for its high acidity and tannins, floral perfume, wild berry fruit and savoury edge. It's a brilliant match for the layered flavours here – the rose harissa's spice and perfume, the pistachios' nutty warmth and lamb's umami depth. The smoky char from the grilled cutlets echoes the wine's earthy undertones. Xinomavro's pleasantly grippy tannins hold their own against the lamb fat, while its acidity brings freshness and lift. The top region in Greece for Xinomavro is Naoussa – and this is just the dish to showcase the depth and character of this complex red.

For the marinade, combine the yogurt, harissa, garlic, lemon zest, salt and olive oil in a small bowl. Brush the mixture over the lamb flesh, avoiding the bones where possible.

Preheat the grill to high.

Place the ground pistachios on a plate and press the individual cutlets into the nuts, coating lightly on both sides. Place the lamb in an ovenproof dish and cook under the grill for 3–4 minutes on each side for medium-rare, until slightly charred on the outside but still tender within.

Allow to rest for 10–15 minutes before serving with flatbreads warmed under the grill, lashing of tzatziki and a pea, mint, radish and pomegranate salad.

OTHER WINES

Similar fragrant, structured wines, such as those made from the grape Nebbiolo (Barolo or Barbaresco). For dark fruit and savoury undertones, Austrian Blaufränkisch, or the floral and expressive Zweigelt, also from Austria.

VEGETARIAN & CHEESE

Soave with pesto pasta

SERVES 4

60g (2¼oz) pine nuts

40g (1½oz) basil leaves

2 small garlic cloves

45g (1¾oz) Parmesan cheese, grated, plus extra to serve

45g (1¾oz) Pecorino Romano cheese, grated

8 tablespoons extra virgin olive oil, plus extra to drizzle

zest and juice of ½ lemon

300g (10½oz) dried pasta

salt

Soave is finally getting the attention it deserves – especially at the premium end – and is now being mentioned in the same breath as some of the world's top white wine regions. Hailing from northeastern Italy's Veneto region, it's made primarily from Garganega – not the most glamorous-sounding grape, but the wine tells a different story: stone fruit, almond, citrus zest, garden flowers and saline freshness. Soave is elegant and food-friendly, working wonders with veggie and pasta dishes – like this simple pesto pasta. Here the umami depth from Parmesan and pine nuts echoes Soave's subtle nutty edge. The wine's citrus brightness and fresh acidity lift the dish and cut through the oily texture of the pesto. Bottles labelled just 'Soave' can still offer great value, but trade up to Soave Classico for more depth, complexity and even some ageing potential.

Begin by toasting the pine nuts in a dry frying pan over a medium heat, stirring often, until lightly golden. Set aside one-third of them for garnish.

Place the remaining pine nuts in a blender with the basil, garlic, Parmesan, Pecorino, olive oil and lemon juice. Blitz to your desired consistency – very smooth or slightly coarse. Season to taste.

Cook the pasta according to the packet instructions, then drain, reserving some of the cooking water. Stir the pesto through the pasta, adding a little of the reserved pasta water to loosen the dish. Serve topped with the toasted pine nuts, lemon zest, a drizzle of oil and an extra shaving of Parmesan.

OTHER WINES

Unoaked Italian white with citrus depth, such as Verdicchio, Gavi – or, for a little more texture and ripeness, Fiano or Greco from the south. Over the border in France, Chablis always works, as do simple fresh sparkling wines, such as Prosecco.

Sauvignon Blanc with pea and asparagus frittata

SERVES 4 AS A LIGHT MAIN

150g (5½oz) frozen peas

125g (4½oz) asparagus tips

8 eggs

dash of groundnut oil

100g (3½oz) feta cheese, crumbled

zest of ½ lemon

1 tablespoon finely chopped flat leaf parsley

salt and pepper

Eggs, peas and asparagus can pose a challenge when it comes to wine pairing because of their strong green flavours, plenty of umami and a touch of bitterness. But Sauvignon Blanc rises to the challenge – its grassy, herbaceous notes mirror the veg, and its citrusy zest brings freshness and lift. The wine's bright acidity cuts through the richness of the eggs, balancing everything out. In this simple frittata I've got a little feta too, which draws out that flinty mineral edge of Sauvignon Blanc. Just the pick for a brunch or light lunch pairing – a delightful balance of comforting food and zingy energetic wine.

Preheat the oven to 200°C (180°C fan), 400°F, Gas Mark 6.

Blanch the frozen peas and asparagus tips in a saucepan of boiling water for 2 minutes, then drain, rinse in cold water and set aside.

In a mixing bowl, crack the eggs and whisk until uniform. Season with a little salt and pepper.

Heat a little oil over a medium heat in an ovenproof frying pan and pour in the egg mixture. As the egg slowly begins to set (after 2–3 minutes), scatter the blanched asparagus tips and the peas over the top. After another minute, turn off the heat, crumble over the feta and place the pan in the oven. Cook until the feta starts to brown and the egg is set. Scatter with lemon zest and flat leaf parsley before serving.

OTHER WINES

Zesty and fresh white wines, such as Spanish Rueda, English Bacchus and light styles of Furmint. Also dry styles of traditional-method sparkling wine, such as Cava (look for *Brut Nature* on the label).

Nebbiolo with mushroom and truffle tagliatelle

SERVES 4 AS A MAIN

40g (1½oz) dried porcini mushrooms

300ml (10fl oz) boiling water

2 tablespoons olive oil

50g (1¾oz) unsalted butter

400g (14oz) mixed fresh mushrooms (chanterelle, oyster, chestnut), sliced

1 teaspoon thyme leaves

2 garlic cloves, thinly sliced

300g (10½oz) dried tagliatelle

100g (3½oz) Pecorino Romano cheese, grated

salt and black pepper

truffle oil or fresh black truffle, to serve

Savoury and perfumed, Nebbiolo naturally sings alongside mushrooms and truffle. It's a classic case of 'what grows together, goes together' – Piedmont is Nebbiolo's native land and home to some of the world's finest truffles. This tagliatelle is a dreamy match for the grape's seductive profile: the mushrooms, truffle and Parmesan bring layers of umami that echo the wine's fragrant depth. There's balance in the boldness – Nebbiolo's firm tannins meet the rich, starchy elements in the pasta, while its high acidity brings freshness. Earthy meets earthy, and the result will transport you to the Piedmontese hills. Barolo and Barbaresco offer the most refined expressions, but for a more affordable bottle, look to the broader Langhe region.

Place the porcini and boiling water in a bowl and leave to soak for 10 minutes. Drain, reserving the liquid, and finely chop the mushrooms.

Meanwhile, heat the olive oil and a small knob of the butter in a frying pan on a medium heat. Add the fresh mushrooms and cook for 10 minutes. Add the porcini, thyme and garlic and cook for 1 minute.

Strain the reserved mushroom soaking liquid (it will be gritty) through a fine sieve lined with a sheet of kitchen paper into the pan, then take off the heat while you cook the pasta.

Cook the tagliatelle according to the packet instructions, then drain, reserving some of the cooking water. Add both to the mushroom pan with the grated Pecorino and remaining butter. Stir gently until glossy, then serve with a drizzle of truffle oil or fresh truffle shavings.

OTHER WINES

Staying in Italy, Chianti Classico offers both fruity and savoury flavours with high acidity. Earthy styles of Pinot Noir from Burgundy or cool climates such as Oregon give a similar impression, or try a Loire Cabernet Franc, which is great with vegetarian dishes.

Pinot Grigio with grilled peach, pine nut and ricotta salad

SERVES 2–4 AS A LIGHT MAIN

1 tablespoon extra virgin olive oil, plus extra for frying and brushing

50g (1¾oz) pine nuts

4 ripe peaches, stoned and quartered

250g (9oz) ricotta cheese

zest of ½ lemon, plus a squeeze of juice

½ teaspoon flaky sea salt

2–3 Baby Gem lettuces, leaves separated

rosemary focaccia, to serve

For the honey vinaigrette

3 tablespoons olive oil

1 tablespoon white wine vinegar

1 teaspoon runny honey

juice of ½ lemon

1 teaspoon Dijon mustard

½ teaspoon flaky sea salt

½ teaspoon cracked black pepper

This salad calls for a more expressive style of Pinot Grigio, like those from Friuli or Alto Adige (or a Pinot Gris from Alsace in France, Oregon or New Zealand) – one with a bit more character, with ripe orchard fruit but still that signature crisp freshness. A style with a touch of sweetness, in that off-dry category, can work well here, picking up the caramelized nuances of the grilled peach. There's a lovely muddle of flavours here – smoky fruit, toasted nuts and whipped ricotta – a soft play of sweet, savoury and fat. The wine's acidity lifts the richness of the cheese and there's a gentle echo between the grilled fruit and flavours found in these richer styles of Pinot Grigio.

Heat a little olive oil in a frying pan on a medium heat, add the pine nuts and toast with a pinch of flaky sea salt, stirring frequently, until golden. Remove from the pan and set aside.

Brush the peach pieces with a little olive oil. Heat the frying pan over a high heat and cook the peaches in batches until the fruit takes on colour. Remove from the pan and set aside.

Blend the ricotta, lemon zest, 1 tablespoon of olive oil and ½ teaspoon of sea salt flakes in a food processor until light and airy.

Combine all the vinaigrette ingredients in a jar and shake well to emulsify.

To serve, arrange the lettuce leaves on plates, spoon on the whipped ricotta, nestle in the peaches and finish with a scattering of pine nuts and a generous drizzle of the dressing. Serve with warmed focaccia.

OTHER WINES

Peach or floral fresh white wines, such as Chenin Blanc; youthful styles of Viognier or Italian Gavi.

Orange wine with fried gnocchi, sage and butternut

SERVES 2 AS A MAIN

400g (14oz) peeled butternut squash, diced into small cubes

olive oil

grapeseed or other flavourless oil

2 tablespoons capers

20 sage leaves

400g (14oz) fresh gnocchi

40g (1½oz) unsalted butter

zest of ½ lemon

salt and pepper

The first time I tried pan-fried gnocchi was a mini revelation – what a glorious upgrade, with its crisp edges, tender centre and deeper, nuttier flavour. It's a natural match for orange wine, which shares that textural weight and savoury edge. This pairing brings comfort and complexity, offering a layered sensory hit in both the glass and the dish. The bold flavours can handle a range of orange wine styles, from lighter, golden-hued examples to the weightier, more structured and pronounced styles made from extended skin contact. There's flavour synergy in the earthy elements – squash, sage – with a touch of sweetness from the squash adding balance. The rounded mouthfeel in both wine and gnocchi is lifted by citrus zest, capers and the wine's acidity.

Preheat the oven to 220°C (200°C fan), 425°F, Gas Mark 7.

Place the squash in an ovenproof dish, drizzle with olive oil, season with salt and pepper and roast for 20–25 minutes, until coloured but still firm.

Heat a little grapeseed oil in a frying pan over a medium heat and fry the capers for 1–2 minutes, until crisp, then set aside on kitchen paper. Repeat with the sage leaves, frying for 30–60 seconds, until crisp, then set aside.

In the same pan, add a little olive oil if needed and fry the gnocchi over a medium heat for 5–7 minutes, until lightly golden, adding the butter for the final 2 minutes. Season to taste.

Turn off the heat, stir through the roasted squash and plate up. Scatter over the sage, capers and a little lemon zest to finish.

OTHER WINES

Textured and rich white wines, such as Viognier and other Rhône white wines. Ripe, oaked styles of Chardonnay, such as those from Napa Valley (California, USA) and similarly rich styles of Chenin Blanc. Also try light, fragrant red wines with high acidity, such as Pinot Noir.

Frappato with tomato tart

SERVES 4 AS A STARTER,
2 AS A MAIN

1 sheet of ready-rolled puff pastry

250g (9oz) heritage tomatoes in a variety of colours

100g (3½oz) mascarpone cheese

100g (3½oz) ricotta cheese

1 teaspoon dried oregano

zest of ¼ lemon

olive oil

1 egg, beaten

salt and pepper

If you haven't met Frappato yet, let me introduce you to this vibrant, high-quality Sicilian red grape. Light in body but full of energy, it's known for juicy red fruit, soft tannins and mouth-watering acidity. Served lightly chilled, it's a delicious match for this recipe – the tartness of the tomatoes and brightness of the wine play off each other nicely, while its acidity cuts through the creamy base. I also love the textural contrast – crisp pastry, juicy tomatoes, and the silky body of the Frappato all working together in a really satisfying way.

Preheat the oven to 200°C (180°C fan), 400°F, Gas Mark 6, and take the puff pastry out of the fridge 20 minutes before using, so it's easier to unroll.

Unroll the pastry on a lined baking tray and use a blunt knife to score a border around the sides, about 1cm (½ inch) in from the edges. Make a few pricks in the middle of the pastry with a fork, then return to the fridge while you prepare the filling.

Thinly slice the tomatoes and drain on kitchen paper. Mix the mascarpone, ricotta, oregano and lemon zest in a bowl and spread evenly over the pastry, avoiding the borders. Arrange the tomatoes in a single layer on top – I like to do this in colour order, going from dark red to light red, orange, yellow and then green. Drizzle with olive oil and season with salt and pepper.

Brush the border of the puff pastry with the beaten egg and bake in the oven for 20–25 minutes, until the pastry is golden and the tomatoes roasted.

OTHER WINES

Light, fruit-forward red wines with high acidity – my picks are Valpolicella Classico or a light style of Cinsault. Crisp white wines, such as Picpoul de Pinet, Albariño or Assyrtiko, or dry sherries, such as Manzanilla or Fino.

Champagne with mac and cheese

SERVES 4 AS A MAIN

300g (10½oz) dried macaroni

115g (4oz) unsalted butter

90g (3¼oz) plain flour (all-purpose flour)

800ml (28fl oz) whole milk

225g (8oz) Comté cheese, grated

100g (3½oz) Parmesan cheese, grated

½ teaspoon grated nutmeg

1 tablespoon Dijon mustard

60g (2¼oz) panko breadcrumbs

zest of 1 lemon

salt and pepper

finely chopped chives, to garnish

This indulgent pairing is where a little luxe meets a little laid-back. It's a great one for a kitchen supper, elevated by the pop of bubbles, but also works brilliantly served in small bowls at a drinks party. There's something about that playful contrast between the fine and the familiar that people love. Champagne's crisp mousse cuts through the richness of the cheese, while the salt in the dish enhances the wine's vibrancy and mineral edge. There's also a savoury link – the umami depth of aged cheese meets the lees-aged complexity in the Champagne. My pick is a rich style of Blanc de Blancs to match the flavour intensity of the dish, while bringing vivacious acidity and lift.

Preheat the oven to 200°C (180°C fan), 400°F, Gas Mark 6.

Cook the pasta according to the packet instructions for about half the recommended time. Drain and set aside.

Melt the butter in a saucepan over a medium heat. Stir in the flour and cook for 1–2 minutes to form a roux. Gradually whisk in the milk and cook the sauce gently until smooth and thickened. Stir in the cheeses until melted, then season with nutmeg, mustard, salt and pepper. Add the pasta to the sauce and mix well, then transfer to an ovenproof dish.

Combine the panko and lemon zest, then scatter over the top of the mac and cheese and bake for 20 minutes, until golden. Finish with chopped chives.

OTHER WINES

Quality traditional-method sparkling wines, such as English and Franciacorta examples. Chardonnay from Burgundy or cool-climate coastal California (Sonoma or Santa Barbara), balancing fruit, oak or mineral freshness.

Rosé with burrata, strawberries and tomatoes

SERVES 4 AS A STARTER

300g (10½oz) strawberries

300g (10½oz) large ripe tomatoes

2 fresh burrata cheeses

60g (2¼oz) basil, leaves picked

2 teaspoons red wine vinegar

4 teaspoons olive oil

2 teaspoons water

1 teaspoon salt

cracked black pepper

A playful take on the classic pairing of strawberries and cream. Juicy fresh strawberries and tomatoes sit alongside creamy burrata, with a chilled rosé that picks up on the bright berry and fruit notes. The sweetness of the strawberries and tomatoes complements the red-fruited profile of the rosé, while its acidity cuts through the richness of the cheese. There's a lovely textural contrast too – the soft, indulgent burrata against the crisp, dry finish of the rosé. A herby basil dressing adds lift and fragrance, working particularly well with mineral, floral-leaning rosés. My pick would be a cool-climate style with plenty of vibrancy and acidity – something from England or the Loire Valley.

Prepare the strawberries by washing and patting them dry, then slice and dice some, keeping the greenery on the smaller ones. Repeat with the tomatoes, cutting them into bite-sized chunks and slices.

Scatter the strawberries and tomatoes on a serving plate and nestle a burrata at either end, opening one of the burrata so that its creamy centre oozes out. Scatter one-third of the basil leaves over the salad.

To make the dressing, blitz the remaining basil with the vinegar, olive oil, water and salt in a blender. Drizzle over the burratas and a little over the tomatoes. Finish with cracked black pepper.

OTHER WINES

Light and fresh sparkling rosés with fresh red berry fruit and high acidity, such as Cava rosado and French rosé Crémants from Loire and Languedoc.

Gavi with orzo, courgette, almond, lemon and chilli

SERVES 4 AS A MAIN

3 courgettes (zucchini), mixed yellow and green, if available, very finely sliced

1 teaspoon lemon thyme leaves

1 teaspoon dried oregano

1 red chilli, finely chopped, or a pinch of dried chilli flakes (red pepper flakes)

3 tablespoons smoked salted almonds, roughly chopped

3 tablespoons olive oil, plus extra for drizzling

300g (10½oz) dried orzo

zest and juice of 1 lemon

salt and pepper

A simple pasta pairing that's unfussy, satisfying and built mostly from cupboard staples – ideal for a casual supper. Gavi has long been a go-to of mine for relaxed, crowd-pleasing meals. It's the kind of wine everyone seems to like – fresh, unoaked, easy-going and versatile with food. Made from the Cortese grape in northern Italy, this citrusy white has gentle nutty undertones, bright acidity and a clean, mineral finish – great with salads, veggie dishes or light pasta. Here, the lemon and lemon thyme in the orzo pick up the wine's zesty character, while the slight bitterness from the courgette and almonds is lifted by these qualities. I love the play between the grainy texture of the orzo and the wine's crispness – and there's a natural link in the citrus, green and nutty notes running through both.

Preheat the oven to 180°C (160°C fan), 350°F, Gas Mark 4.

Line a baking tray with nonstick baking paper and arrange the courgettes on it in a single layer. Sprinkle with the lemon thyme, dried oregano and chilli, and finish by scattering with the smoked salted almonds and the olive oil. Roast for 5 minutes to soften.

Meanwhile, cook the pasta according to the packet instructions, then drain, reserving some of the cooking water. Return it to the pan with a little of the reserved water and add the roasted courgette mix, gently tossing everything together. To serve, add the lemon zest and juice and some black pepper and top with an extra drizzle of olive oil.

OTHER WINES

Bright Italian white wines, such as Soave or Verdicchio. Similar whites from further afield, such as Picpoul de Pinet, Albariño or dry Furmint.

SWEET

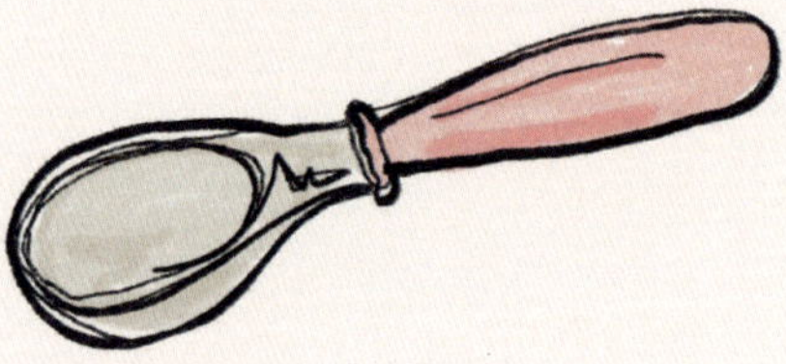

Tawny Port with rocky road 172

Sauternes with griddled pineapple, ice cream and honeyed nuts 175

Tokaji with apricot tarte Tatin 176

Moscato d'Asti with white chocolate rainbow bark 179

Tawny Port with rocky road

SERVES 10–12

100g (3½oz) hazelnuts

300g (10½oz) dark (bittersweet) chocolate (70%), broken into small pieces

75g (2¾oz) unsalted butter

2 tablespoons tawny Port

75g (2¾oz) amaretti biscuits, roughly broken

150g (5½oz) dried figs, chopped

flaky sea salt

There's no need to save Port for a formal cheese board or fancy dinner – it's just as brilliant with the simplest of sweet things, especially chocolate. While ruby styles are the traditional match with chocolate, I've got a soft spot for tawny Port – all mellow, nutty and caramelized – maybe because I grew up on fruit and nut chocolate bars. The rocky road here has had a bit of a glow-up – a splash of Port, amaretti biscuits, dried figs and toasted hazelnuts – all nodding to the flavours in the glass. Decidedly spoiling, but still relaxed, it's a modern, indulgent way to enjoy this historic fortified wine. Go for a tawny with a bit of age – at least ten years – for that nutty depth.

Begin by lining a loaf tin (about 20 x 10cm/8 x 4 inches) or a square tin (about 18cm/7 inches) with nonstick baking paper.

Toast the hazelnuts in a dry frying pan over a medium heat for 2–3 minutes, until golden. Allow to cool, then chop roughly.

Place the chocolate and butter in a heatproof bowl set over a saucepan of gently simmering water and stir until melted and smooth. Remove immediately from the heat. Add a pinch of flaky sea salt, stir in the Port and fold in the amaretti, figs and hazelnuts. Transfer the mixture to the lined tin and press down evenly. Refrigerate for at least 2 hours, then slice to serve.

OTHER WINES

Sweet, fortified wines, such as Pedro Ximénez Sherry or a sweet Oloroso Sherry, Banyuls from France, the sweeter Bual or Malmsey styles of Madeira, or Rutherglen Muscat from Australia.

Sauternes with griddled pineapple, ice cream and honeyed nuts

SERVES 4

100g (3½oz) caster sugar (superfine sugar)

50g (1¾oz) mixed nuts, roughly chopped

pinch of flaky sea salt

pinch of ground cinnamon

1 pineapple, cored and sliced into 1cm (½ inch) rings

4 scoops of vanilla ice cream

zest of ½ orange

Liquid gold. Totally hedonistic. Moreishly decadent. There's something about Sauternes – the world's most famous sweet wine from Bordeaux – that always leaves an impression. For me, it always brings a knowing smile. Made from botrytized (noble rot-affected) grapes, Semillon with a lift from Sauvignon Blanc and Muscadelle, and aged in oak, it delivers unctuous layers of honeyed fruit, sweetness and gentle spice. This dessert pairing is a tribute to all that deliciousness: the pineapple's caramelization, orange zest and nuts mirror the wine's noble rot characteristics, and the vanilla ice cream picks up on similar notes from oak contact. Crucially, the racy acidity on the finish keeps the sweetness in check and everything feeling lifted.

Place the caster sugar in a medium pan on a low-medium heat. Once the sugar has dissolved, add a splash of water and turn the heat to high until the mixture begins to boil. Swirling the pan occasionally, cook until it turns golden brown, then remove quickly from the heat and stir in the nuts, salt and cinnamon. Pour onto a baking tray lined with nonstick baking paper and leave to cool, then break into pieces.

Heat a griddle or frying pan on a high heat and cook the pineapple rings in batches until lightly caramelized.

Arrange 2 or 3 slices of pineapple on each plate with a scoop of vanilla ice cream. Top with the honeyed nut crumb and finish with a little grated orange zest.

OTHER WINES

Similar rich, sweet white wines, such as Tokaji (look for *Aszu* on the label for a similarly unctuous style made from noble rot-affected grapes). Sweet Chenin Blancs from the Loire Valley, such as those from Côteaux du Layon. Late-harvest Riesling. Sweet Semillon from Australia.

Tokaji with apricot tarte Tatin

SERVES 4–6

1 sheet of ready-rolled all-butter puff pastry

30g (1oz) salted butter

a few sprigs of thyme, plus extra to decorate

2 tablespoons sugar

8–10 ripe apricots, halved and stoned

crème fraîche or vanilla ice cream, to serve

This dessert brings back such fond memories – my mum would make it on holiday with delicious, ripe apricots, gently cooked in butter and sugar. Sometimes it was a tad too caramelized, or a bit rough around the edges – but that didn't matter. There's something so special about a homemade tart made with love. Tokaji, Hungary's famous sweet wine, has a natural affinity with desserts like this. Its vibrant acidity lifts the richness of the fruit and pastry, while its honeyed, marmalade and ginger notes – thanks to grapes affected by noble rot – play beautifully with the caramelized apricots. For a lighter, fresher, more floral style of sweet wine from the same region, look for late-harvest Tokaji.

Preheat the oven to 200°C (180°C fan), 400°F, Gas Mark 6, and take the puff pastry out of the fridge 20 minutes before using, so it's easier to unroll.

Melt the butter in a small ovenproof frying pan on a low heat. Add the thyme and sugar and allow it to slowly start bubbling. Arrange the apricots in the pan, cut sides down, and cook gently for about 15 minutes so they begin to caramelize.

Unroll the pastry and cut a disc to fit the pan. Gently place it over the fruit, moulding it around the apricots. Bake for about 25 minutes, until golden. Rest for about 10 minutes, then gently run a knife around the edge and invert carefully onto a plate. Top with a few thyme sprigs and serve warm with crème fraîche or vanilla ice cream.

OTHER WINES

White sweet wines, including sweet styles of Chenin from the Loire Valley, such as Coteaux du Layon. Sweet Sauternes from Bordeaux. Italian Vin Santo. *Demi-sec* Champagne.

Moscato d'Asti with white chocolate rainbow bark

SERVES 6

200g (7oz) good-quality white chocolate, broken into small pieces

flaky sea salt

Suggestions for toppings

strawberries

mango

kiwi

blueberries

passion fruit

pistachios

edible flowers

Moscato d'Asti is a playful dessert wine, low in alcohol with a gentle tickle of bubbles. Sweet, floral and full of charm, it's often overlooked in favour of 'serious' dessert wines, but it really shouldn't be. It brings something light and fragrant and is a genuinely joyful finale – which, frankly, is often exactly what's needed. This pairing leans into that bright and relaxed vibe: bold flavour without weight, fruit and florals in both bark and the wine; and even a spritz of passionfruit to echo the wine's gentle fizz. A fresh and uplifting happy ending that tastes as delicious as it looks.

Line a baking tray with nonstick baking paper. Place the chocolate in a heatproof bowl set over a saucepan of gently simmering water and stir until melted and smooth. Remove immediately from the heat and allow to cool a little. Fold in a pinch of salt and spread the chocolate into the lined tray in a layer 3–5mm (⅛–¼ inch) thick.

Top the chocolate with your chosen fruit, nuts and edible flowers, then freeze for 1 hour, until solid. Break the bark into shards and serve immediately with an optional extra pinch of salt.

OTHER WINES

Demi-sec styles of sparkling wine, such as Champagne or sweeter Crémant from the Loire Valley. Sweeter styles of Riesling (typically labelled *Spätlese* or *Auslese*). Sweeter or late-harvest styles of Chenin Blanc. Sweet and pure ice wine from Canada or Germany (*Eiswein*).

PART 3

CURATE

CURATED WINE EXPERIENCES TO ENJOY AT HOME

This section explores themes, menus and ideas for wine-focused entertaining. We start with seasonal themes – spring, summer, autumn and winter – then move on to two style-focused occasions, sparkling wine and rosé. From there, I share some of my favourite wine moments, from casual takeout to cheese and wine, the canned fish phenomenon, and tips for hosting everything from brunch to a full-blown party. The final themes focus on menus inspired by some of my favourite wine regions and countries.

A SPRING THING

Spring brings into focus bright and lifted ingredients, as well as tender meats, making it a delight to pair with fresh and characterful wines. Here are some key ingredients and flavours for spring with wine considerations.

Fresh, green, aromatic vegetables and herbs
Think peas, asparagus, watercress, wild garlic, dill, radishes and sorrel. They sing with zippy whites, such as Sauvignon Blanc, Grüner Veltliner and English Bacchus, where citrus and herbal bite mirror the green edge. Non-vintage traditional-method sparkling wines work too, bringing freshness with a subtle biscuity backbone. Where vegetables have a little sweetness – peas especially – go for rounder whites, such as Chenin Blanc or Soave Classico.

Umami-forward vegetables
Artichokes and morels are great with high-acid whites with depth, such as lightly oaked Chardonnay, to give lift. Light reds with a savoury edge, such as Pinot Noir, also work beautifully.

Tender meats
Lamb and spring chicken are in season, and at this time of year they are lovely cooked with lemon, herbs and new-season veg rather than in heavy stews. Pair lamb with bright, modern reds that balance fruit and freshness. I particularly like Loire Cabernet Franc and contemporary, less alcoholic Rhône reds (look for less than 13.5% ABV). Spring chicken is versatile, suiting everything from rosé, orange, white or red.

Tangy spring fruit
Rhubarb gives tart vibrancy or, when sweetened, a softer flavour. Both styles work with wines with sweetness. Savoury-leaning rhubarb dishes – for example with ricotta – pair well with off-dry rosés, such as Rosé d'Anjou. Sweet rhubarb desserts can pair nicely with aromatic wines, such as Gewürztraminer, where lychee, floral and spice notes shine.

MENU IDEAS

Starters

- **Asparagus tempura with miso mayonnaise** – Loire Sauvignon Blanc (Sancerre, Pouilly-Fumé, Touraine)
- **Pea and mint soup** – Soave Classico
- **Braised artichokes** – White Burgundy (Bourgogne, Mâconnais or for premium styles, see villages in the Côte de Beaune), or similar cool-climate styles from USA, South Africa, Australia or New Zealand

Mains

- **Butterflied leg of lamb** – Cabernet Franc from the Loire (such as Chinon) or from the Finger Lakes, New York
- **Spring chicken with morels** – Chenin Blanc, such as dry Vouvray from the Loire or old-vine styles from South Africa
- **Salmon en croute** – Unoaked or lightly oaked Chardonnay, such as Chablis or similar styles from cool regions in the USA, South Africa, Australia or New Zealand

Desserts

- **Rhubarb crumble** – Sweet German Rieslings (look for Kabinett on the label and the ABV will usually be under 10%)
- **Lemon tart** – Moscato d'Asti
- **Ricotta and honey tart** – Vin Santo (Italian speciality sweet wine)

Spring-inspired recipes in this book

- Sauvignon Blanc with a veggie platter and whipped feta dip (see page 78)
- Sauvignon Blanc with pea and asparagus frittata (see page 154)
- Grüner Veltliner with a herby trout salad (see page 110)
- Xinomavro with harissa lamb cutlets and pistachio (see page 148)

SUMMER SIPS

Summer cooking is all about freshness, simplicity and sunshine flavours. Think vibrant plates and plenty of produce eaten outdoors, with wines that are crisp and easy to drink: bright whites and rosés, sparkling wines or chilled lighter reds.

Sun-ripened, juicy vegetables

Raw, fresh tomato dishes shine with crisp, high-acid whites and rosés. For baked tomato flavours, try light reds, such as Frappato or Valpolicella Classico. With other summer veg, such as peppers, courgettes (zucchini) and cucumber, consider the preparation: keep it bright with citrusy whites if served simply, or move to bolder wines – oaked Chardonnay or light reds with a green edge, such as Cabernet Franc or Mencía – for stuffed or baked dishes.

Mediterranean and aromatic herbs

Mediterranean herbs, such as basil, oregano and thyme, are echoed in many southern French reds (Grenache-Syrah-Mourvèdre blends), Spanish Rioja and Italian Sangiovese. Aromatic herbs, such as coriander (cilantro), lift beautifully with white grapes – Sauvignon Blanc, Riesling or Grüner Veltliner, for example.

Grilled protein

Prawns (shrimp), sardines, mackerel, chicken and lightly seasoned red meats pair well with medium-intensity wines. My go-to picks are Mediterranean rosé for both meat and fish, and light reds, such as Pinot Noir, or smoky Rhône Syrah for grilled meats. For seafood, medium-oaked Chardonnay, Albariño and Assyrtiko are all excellent matches.

Ripe summer fruits

Strawberries, raspberries, cherries, peaches and nectarines are best with wines that mirror their sweetness. Red fruit desserts pair with Moscato d'Asti or Brachetto (a lightly sparkling sweet red). Stone fruit puddings shine with sweet Chenin Blanc – think Vouvray or Coteaux du Layon from the Loire, or late-harvest South African styles.

MENU IDEAS

Starters

- **Grilled sardines with lemon and herbs** – Albariño
- **Watermelon and feta salad with mint** – Assyrtiko
- **Tomato bruschetta with olive oil and garlic** – Provence rosé

Mains

- **Herby barbecue chicken** – Côtes du Rhône Blanc
- **Grilled whole sea bass** – Chablis (unoaked Chardonnay)
- **Stuffed peppers with rice and halloumi** – Valpolicella Classico

Desserts

- **Strawberries and cream** – Loire Rosé d'Anjou
- **Peach and almond pavlova** – Late-harvest Chenin Blanc (Loire or South Africa)
- **Basil ice cream with biscotti** – Gewürztraminer, especially sweeter styles, such as Vendanges Tardives (VT) styles from Alsace

Summer-inspired recipes in this book

- Vinho Verde with fish tacos (see page 106)
- Frappato with tomato tart (see page 162)
- Gavi with orzo, courgette, almond, lemon and chilli (see page 169)
- Cabernet Franc with pork and Padrón pepper kebabs (see page 136)

AUTUMN POURS

Autumn brings warmth and richness – earthy vegetables, orchard fruit, game and slow-cooked dishes. Wines that meet these flavours with depth, balancing acidity and an echo of that earthiness, are great picks.

Earthy and umami-rich vegetables
Mushrooms (ceps, chanterelles, truffles), pumpkin and squash work well with fruit-forward wines that also carry depth and acidity to balance savoury elements, or wines with umami notes for synergy. Pinot Noir and Nebbiolo are classics with mushrooms and truffles, as are complex Champagnes and aged Chardonnay. For pumpkin and squash, look to textured whites from the Rhône (Marsanne, Roussanne, Viognier) or rich styles of Chenin Blanc.

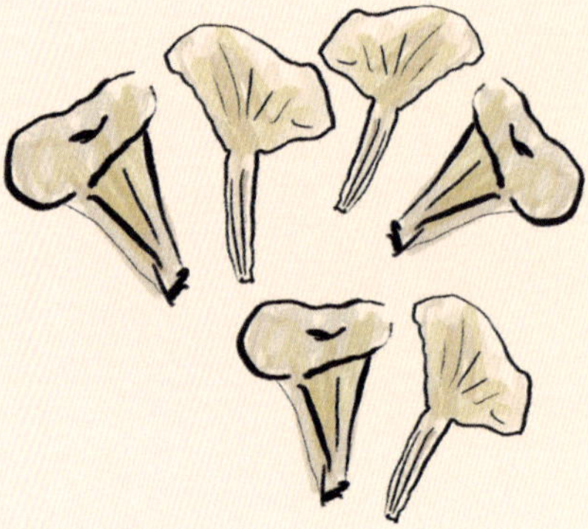

Game and richer meats
Venison, lamb, duck, pheasant and guinea fowl are naturally high in umami, so suit reds with savoury complexity – think Pinot Noir, Nebbiolo or mature Rioja. For richer cuts also consider the opulent Amarone della Valpolicella or muscular Aglianico (both from Italy), Grenache-Syrah-Mourvèdre blends or Cabernet Sauvignon from Bordeaux or further afield. Many of these dishes lend themselves to slow cooking, which softens the meat and concentrates flavour, making them even better with structured, full-bodied wines.

Orchard fruit
Desserts containing apples, pears, quinces and figs are wonderful with classic botrytized wines (Sauternes, Tokaji) or late-harvest styles of Riesling or Chenin Blanc.

MENU IDEAS

Starters

- **Truffle arancini** – Franciacorta
- **Roasted fig and goats' cheese tart** – Off-dry Chenin Blanc (Loire, such as certain styles of Vouvray)
- **Wild mushrooms on grilled sourdough** – Pinot Noir (such as Burgundy, Oregon, New Zealand)

Mains

- **Moroccan lamb tagine** – Rhône Grenache-Syrah-Mourvèdre blend
- **Butternut squash lasagne** – Viognier (Rhône or USA)
- **Roast venison with red wine jus** – Amarone della Valpolicella

Desserts

- **Poached pears** – Sauternes
- **Pumpkin pie** – Tokaji
- **Apple crumble** – Sweet Chenin Blanc

Autumn-inspired recipes in this book

- Viognier with chicken and pumpkin pie (see page 127)
- Chenin Blanc with honey and miso pork belly (see page 139)
- Nebbiolo with mushroom and truffle tagliatelle (see page 157)

WINTER WARMERS

Winter calls for comfort and generosity – robust meats, strong cheeses, rich sauces and warming spices. Wines with structure, weight and intensity shine here, whether bold reds, opulent whites or lusciously sweet styles.

Deep and rich proteins

Beef, stews, shellfish, salt cod, duck and turkey call for wines with matching weight and intensity. With fish and shellfish, think complex sparkling wines, dry Sherries or oaked whites. For game, see the suggestions for Autumn (see page 188), while turkey is excellent with quality, structured Beaujolais, aged Bordeaux reds or Rhône blends, as well as rich white wines.

Strong dairy and cheese

Blue cheese is a timeless match for Sauternes or Port. Comté, Gruyère and raclette love bold, oaky Chardonnay, the nutty depth of Vin Jaune, or rich dry or off-dry Chenin Blanc.

Warming spices, fruits and nuts

The flavours of cinnamon, ginger, cardamom, dried figs, dates, walnuts and chestnuts echo beautifully in certain wines. Grenache and Grenache-dominant blends (such as Châteauneuf-du-Pape) often show winter spice. Amarone della Valpolicella brings fig, raisin and spice notes, while tawny Port and Pedro Ximénez Sherry offer dried fruit and nut richness. On the white side, Alsatian Pinot Gris can give hints of spice and nuttiness.

MENU IDEAS

Starters

- **Scallops with black pudding** – Blanc de Blancs Champagne
- **Salt cod croquettes** – Manzanilla Sherry
- **Cheese soufflés** – Oaked Chardonnay (from Burgundy or similar styles from other regions)

Mains

- **Beef Wellington** – Bordeaux Left Bank (Cabernet Sauvignon dominant) or Napa Valley Cabernet Sauvignon
- **Confit turkey leg with cranberry sauce** – Cru Beaujolais (such as Fleurie or Morgon)
- **Cauliflower and chickpea curry with cardamom and ginger** – Off-dry Pinot Gris from Alsace

Desserts

- **Pecan pie** – Madeira (Bual or Malmsey)
- **Sticky toffee pudding** – Pedro Ximénez Sherry
- **Chocolate and chestnut torte** – Vintage Port

Winter-inspired recipes in this book

- Picpoul de Pinet with grilled garlic mussels (see page 97)
- Garnacha with warm duck salad (see page 132)
- Tawny Port with rocky road (see page 172)

POP AND POUR

This section is about opening up the perspective of sparkling wine. About not just seeing it as a celebratory toast or aperitif, but as a gastronomic wine, just as capable of charming with flavour and aroma throughout an entire tasting or meal, as much as with its effervescent spirit. A whole evening of bubbles might feel a little unconventional, but it's a wonderful way to explore the breadth and diversity of the style.

The focus here is on traditional-method sparkling wines – first perfected in Champagne (though Limoux in southern France also lays claim), but now crafted across the world.

The two menus that follow set up contrasting evenings. The first is a sit-down dinner showcasing Champagne through matched pairings across each course. The second is a more informal, stand-up-and-nibble sparkling night, comparing styles from around the world.

THE GRAND CHAMPAGNE TOUR

Aperitif

- Non-vintage Grand Marque or Grower Champagne with fish goujons, devilled eggs and caviar (see page 73) or simple snacks, such as briny olives and salty cheese straws.

Starter

- Blanc de Blancs Champagne made from white-only grapes, giving poise, bright acidity, citrus and complexity, which works exceptionally with fish and shellfish, such as scallops and samphire (see page 90).

Main

- Blanc de Noirs or Vintage Champagne (complex, layered and round), served with light red meats, such as honey and miso pork belly (see page 139).

Dessert

- Demi-Sec Champagne (can be a little harder to get hold of, but if you can, it is a total delight) paired with desserts such as classic tarte Tatin or apricot tarte Tatin (see page 176), poached pears or white chocolate.

SPARKLING EXPLORATION

For a fun night of fizzy exploration, line up sparkling wines from different regions across the world. Serve them chilled in a big ice bucket so that guests can dip in and compare styles side by side. For an added element of surprise, slip the bottles into wine socks and pour them blind – it's a brilliant way to spark conversation and see which region comes out as the crowd favourite without letting preconceptions about the region or producer steer opinions.

The menu

For easy hosting, go for casual snacky bites, such as a veggie platter and whipped feta dip (see page 78) alongside indulgent cheese-focused treats such as my mac and cheese (see page 165) or truffled cheese toasties (see page 74), where the bubbles cut through the richness. These wines are also brilliant with fatty meats, fried snacks, such as arancini, or casual fish goujons (see page 73).

The wine list

- **Champagne** – For the benchmark-quality sparkling, serve a Grand Marque Champagne and consider comparing alongside a Grower Champagne.
- **Crémant** – Traditional-method sparkling from France made outside the Champagne region. Softer acidity, slightly gentler bubbles, excellent value. Key regions: Languedoc, Limoux, Alsace.
- **Cava/Corpinnat** – Spanish sparklings; Cava ranges from simple to serious, Corpinnat focuses on quality and indigenous grapes.
- **Franciacorta/Trento** – Northern Italy's finest; Franciacorta (Lombardy) makes richer, rounded, Champagne-like wines, while Trentodoc (Trentino-Alto Adige) makes crisp and fresh styles.
- **Méthode Cap Classique** (South Africa) – Great value, easy-drinking traditional-method wines with soft texture.
- **English sparkling wine** – World-class fizz with bright acidity and complexity; vintage examples often rival Champagne on price and quality.
- **California or Australia** – Traditional-method sparklings with growing prestige. Look out for Anderson Valley (California) and Tasmania (Australia) in particular.

ROSÉ ALL DAY

I'm a big advocate of pink with plates. Yes, nothing beats a chilled, rosé-hued glass poolside or at a beach club – but don't underestimate the foodie potential of rosé. With fruit notes balanced by acidity, a little more body than many whites, but lighter than most reds – plus layers of florals, herbs and mineral tones, depending on grape and region – rosé is incredibly versatile at the table. It works across a feast and often wins over fussy drinkers too.

First, let's explore one of my top tips for pairing with rosé – if in doubt, think pink and match with pink-toned foods. After that we have an interesting comparison of rosé wines from around the world.

THINK PINK

Pink-hued foods pair spectacularly with rosé wines, and they cross the spectrum of seasons – remember rosé isn't just for summer sipping.

- ✦ **Salmon, trout and tuna** – Oily fish with rich and sometimes smoky flavours bring lots of umami, so pair beautifully with the fruit and freshness of rosé.
- ✦ **Lobster, prawn and crab** – Shellfish bring lots of umami but also sweet, delicate and saline notes, echoing many found in rosé.
- ✦ **Pork and duck** – These in-between meats are tender and juicy, with savoury and fatty elements, and are lifted by the fruit and acidity in rosé.
- ✦ **Cured meats** – The salty, savoury and umami qualities are great with rosé for contrast and freshness.
- ✦ **Pomegranate, strawberries, watermelon and pink grapefruit** – These fruity, refreshing and tangy ingredients can be incorporated into salads and other dishes to mirror similar fruit notes in rosé.

Rosé recipes in this book

- ✦ Rosé with beetroot-and-gin-cured salmon (see page 85)
- ✦ Deep-hued rosé with tuna niçoise (see page 113)
- ✦ Provence rosé with spicy salmon skewers (see page 114)

ROSÉ FROM AROUND THE WORLD

For a rosé-themed soirée, let's discover some different styles from around the world. France is the home of this style, and the list below covers four key regions showing the breadth of styles from one country. But beyond France are some other picks from Europe and further afield. Broadly, the wines are listed from lightest to boldest in style, with alternative regions of South Africa and Greece included at the end. This could be a fun sip-and-taste evening, pairing each rosé with different small plates to complement its flavours – I've included some suggestions for delicious paired bites below.

- ✦ **English rosé** – Crisp, high acid and delicate fruit character. Serve with radishes and crudités with salted butter.
- ✦ **Provence rosé** – Pale, very dry, elegant and nuanced fruit. Serve with spicy prawns (shrimp).
- ✦ **Loire rosé** – Crunchy berries, mineral, herbal lift. Serve with trout pâté on crackers.
- ✦ **Spanish Garnacha Rosado** – Ripe, berry fruit, generous body. Serve with pan con tomate.
- ✦ **Tavel rosé** – Deeper in colour, structured, vibrant fruit, full body. Serve with seared tuna bites and tapenade.
- ✦ **Bandol rosé** – Savoury, age-worthy, gastronomic. Serve with lamb kofta skewers.
- ✦ **South African rosé** – Pinotage or Cinsault-based. Serve with bresaola and Parmesan.
- ✦ **Greek rosé** – Xinomavro or Agiorgitiko-based. Serve with grilled halloumi and pomegranate.

TAKEOUT NIGHT

For those evenings when cooking is off the cards, here are my tips for pairing wines with your favourite takeout.

Pizza

Consider the toppings – richer meat-focused toppings can be paired with bolder red wines, whereas veggie toppings are versatile with medium-intense styles of white, red and rosé. For all-rounder picks, look for medium-bodied, fruity, high-acid reds and rosés, such as Barbera (Italy), Côtes du Rhône (France), Provence-style or deeper styles of rosé, such as Spanish Garnacha Rosado.

Indian

Wine pairing will depend on whether the meal focuses on lighter, creamy curries and seafood or rich, meaty curries, plus the level of heat in the dishes. Off-dry Riesling is a winner with the former style, as well as dishes with heat; also consider Chenin Blanc, especially off-dry styles. Fruit-forward styles of Grenache or Spanish Garnacha are versatile with meaty dishes and may echo similar spice notes too.

Chinese

If sticking to light dishes – steamed dim sum, for example – fresh styles of traditional-method sparkling wine, such as Cava or Crémant, are a great pairing. With steamed fish dishes, particularly those packed with ginger and soy and aromatic herbs (such as coriander), dry Riesling or crisp Loire Sauvignon Blanc work well. With duck dishes, light to medium reds balancing fruit and savoury character are perfect, such as Pinot Noir, Blaufränkisch or Gamay (Beaujolais).

Thai

Many Thai dishes combine sweet, spice, salty, sour and aromatic ingredients, including green curry, mango noodle salad and Pad Thai. These are best served with white wines with freshness and a little bit of sweetness too. My picks are off-dry Riesling, fuller styles of Pinot Grigio (typically Pinot Gris from Alsace or quality, rich Italian styles), and sparkling styles of rosé that are on the sweeter end of Brut.

Fish and chips or fried chicken

These foods require wines with energy and acidity to cut through the fat. Fizz always works a treat. At the more luxury end, Champagne and English sparkling wine are great picks, whereas Crémant de Loire or Cava can provide something a bit more affordable. If you are not in the mood for sparkling, then crisp unoaked white wines are also a great option, such as Chardonnay from Chablis, Muscadet or Albariño.

Kebabs

Being all about smoky meats and that lovely bit of char, kebabs work particularly well with reds that balance freshness with a bit of savoury spice. Go-to picks include Rhône-style Syrah, with its peppery edge, Loire Cabernet Franc with its green bell pepper nuances, or red Rioja that can give sweet spice notes from oak.

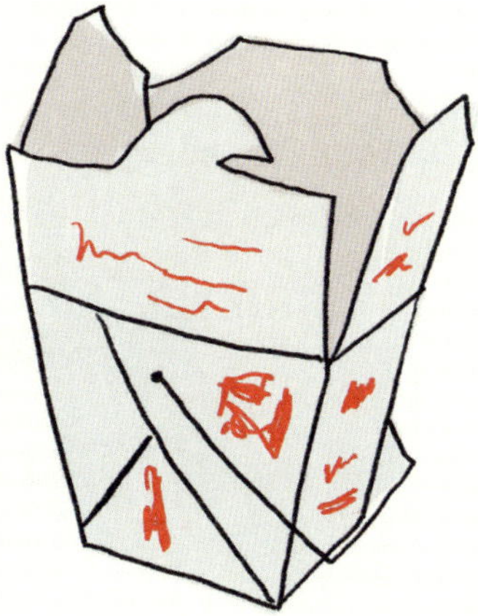

CHEESE AND WINE NIGHT

Cheese and wine night will always be a thing. There's something so glorious about an abundance of delicious cheese, layered on boards – some creamy, some veiny, some ashy, tangy, light, intense – the whole works. Serve with grapes, figs, chutneys, honey, crunchy crackers and crusty bread so that everyone can make up a plate to tuck into with some sumptuous wines.

With its salty and umami character, cheese pairs brilliantly with fruit-driven wines, sweet wines and those that share savoury, umami-like nuances. Cheese is also rich in fat, so it works especially well with wines that have high acidity to cut through that richness and refresh the palate.

If you're looking to keep to three diverse wines that are versatile with a mixed cheese board, my top picks are:

- **Champagne** – Complex and fresh with high acidity, cutting through the fat and giving lift.
- **Sweet Chenin Blanc** – Rounded and honeyed, matching texture and providing a pleasant sweet counterpoint.
- **Gamay** (Beaujolais) – Red-fruited, silky and bright acidity, giving a flavour contrast with red fruit, and freshness to balance fat and texture.

CHEESE AND WINE PARTY

Here's how to host a cheese and wine party: a little nod to the 1970s, but with a modern feel. The following pairings set out excellent matches for each cheese style, listed from mildest to strongest to give a natural order for tasting.

Cheese selection and wine pairings

- **Sauvignon Blanc** (Loire Valley) with goats' cheese
- **Oaked Chardonnay** (Burgundy, Oregon, California or Margaret River, Australia) with bloomy rind cheeses, such as Brie or Camembert
- **Fino** or **Manzanilla Sherry** with Manchego, or Amontillado with aged cheeses
- **Gamay** (Beaujolais) with Comté
- **Sangiovese** (such as Chianti Classico) with Parmesan
- **Champagne** with washed-rind cheese, such as Époisses
- **Sauternes** or **Port** with a blue cheese, such as Stilton

Accompaniments

- Fruit: grapes, ripe figs, pear
- Dried fruit: apricots, dates
- Nuts: walnuts, almonds
- Chutney: fig or onion chutney
- Runny honey
- Crackers: variety of styles, such as water biscuits, seeded crackers, oatcakes
- Bread: crusty baguette or sourdough

Serving tips

Take the cheese out of the fridge at least an hour before serving, allowing for both the flavours to open and textures to soften. Present the wine next to the cheese boards in an ice bucket for guests to help themselves: Gamay is best lightly chilled, while Champagne and white wines should stay cold. If the Sangiovese gets too warm (above about 16°C/61°F), you can return it briefly to the bucket to freshen it up.

TINS AND THINGS

The upmarket tinned fish phenomenon is a modern hosting trend that's here to stay. Introduced to me by my friend Katie for a simple date night or get-together with friends, tinned fish has shed its 'emergency-cupboard' image, and today the most tasteful tins are as much about the contemporary and bright artwork as they are about the taste. Spain and Portugal have paved the way, with high-quality sourcing, careful preparation, and beautifully designed packaging for tuna, anchovies, mussels and more.

Unfussy, quick to put together, stylish to look at – what's not to love about a tinned night in? Pick a few tins, choose a selection of carbs and spreads, and finish with some ingredients for acidity and crunch. Arrange all items over a couple of wooden boards or serving platters and simply tuck in.

When it comes to wines, crisp whites work a treat alongside the mix of umami, salt, acidity, sweetness, bitterness, spice and smoke – plus the combination of smooth and crunchy textures. Here are my top five wine picks, followed by a selection of ingredients to build your own tins and things spread.

Top wine picks with tinned fish

- **Manzanilla or Fino Sherry** (Andalusia, Spain) – Tangy and saline, echoing the sea-saltiness of the fish.
- **Albariño** (Rías Baixas, Spain) – Mineral, fresh, citrusy, cutting through fatty textures.
- **Muscadet** (Loire, France) – Light, crisp and sea-like, a refreshing classic with fish and seafood.
- **Chablis** (Burgundy, France) – Bright, high acidity and a shell-like minerality that lifts smoke and oiliness.
- **Txakoli** (Basque Country, Spain) – Zesty, fresh, with a light spritz; a playful charmer with fishy flavours.

THE PERFECT TINNED FISH SPREAD

Tinned fish

Pick a mix of tins, ideally some fish and some shellfish, prepared in different ways – smoked, spiced, or in olive oil.

- ✦ Sardines
- ✦ Smoked mussels
- ✦ Anchovies
- ✦ Tuna
- ✦ Spiced calamari

Carbs and spreads

Carbs act as the base for your fish, adding texture without overwhelming the flavour, while spreads bring variety from rich and fishy to savoury and veggie.

- ✦ Variety of crackers
- ✦ Toasted sourdough drizzled with olive oil
- ✦ Mackerel pâté
- ✦ Tapenade
- ✦ Salted butter
- ✦ Romesco sauce

Acidity and crunch

These ingredients give the sharp lift needed against fatty, oily and smoky textures, echoing the freshness in the wines.

- ✦ Cornichons
- ✦ Pickled chillies
- ✦ Olives
- ✦ Caperberries
- ✦ Fresh lemon

PARTY TIME

This section provides a checklist for hosting with wine at a drinks party at home, with some tips on which wines to serve and how to serve them.

QUANTITIES

For a drinks party lasting 3–4 hours, where wine is the main serve (with perhaps some beer and non-alcoholic options in the mix), I work on 1–1½ drinks per guest per hour, usually front-loaded at the beginning of the evening. I keep serving sizes small, with 100ml (3½fl oz) pours for sparkling and 150ml (5fl oz) for still wine. If sparkling wine is on offer, that's often sipped first, until it runs out, before guests move to still wine. As a guide, that's around 3–4 glasses of sparkling wine and 2–3 glasses of still wine (split between white, red and possibly rosé) per guest.

It's always good to have a couple of extra bottles in reserve, rather than risk running out, so based on 20 guests, that means:

- ✦ **Sparkling wine** – 8–11 bottles, so round to 12 bottles.
- ✦ **Still wine** – 8–12 bottles, split across red, white and rosé. That's 3–4 bottles of each, so round to 4 bottles of each. Lean quantities more towards white and rosé in the summer.

GLASSWARE

I'd keep to one glass per guest to use for both sparkling and still wine, making an allowance for a few breakages or glasses that go astray. One of my favourite tips at a party is to use a thin chalk marker pen to elegantly (if you can) write the name of each guest on the base. It stops people losing or swapping glasses and the writing washes off easily with water. If you are using one glass for all styles of wine, I'd suggest a universal style with a thin rim and a medium bowl that gently angles inwards (see more on page 216). Don't forget to provide water glasses too.

FORMAT

If you feel like breaking from the norm of standard wine bottles and have the storage or cooler space available, consider magnums (containing the equivalent of two bottles of wine) – they always get guests into the party spirit. Boxed wines are also a great option for still wines, with many high-quality and attractive choices now available, allowing for effortless self-serving.

STORAGE AND SERVING

Keep all wines in the fridge the night before or for at least four hours before the party. Remove red wines from the fridge as guests arrive, keeping them feeling fresh and not too warm by the time they are open. If space permits, keep the other wines in the fridge and serve as you go. I find large ice bins can create a lot of mess, so I prefer to avoid them. Alternatively, a kitchen sink filled with ice and water makes a sensible large cooling bucket. Make sure to have corkscrews at hand for bottles that require them.

WHAT TO SERVE

Sparkling

- **Save** – Cava, Crémant, South African Méthode Cap Classique.
- **Spend** – English sparkling wine, Franciacorta, Tasmania, California.
- **Splurge** – Premium Cava (look for Cava de Paraje Calificado on the label), prestige English sparkling wine and Franciacorta, Champagne from non-vintage through to vintage.

Unoaked, fresh or lightly oaked white wine

- **Save** – Gavi, Verdicchio, Albariño.
- **Spend** – Soave Classico, Assyrtiko, Etna Bianco.
- **Splurge** – Sancerre (Loire, Sauvignon Blanc), Chablis (unoaked Chardonnay), lightly oaked Chardonnay, such as Oregon or white Burgundy.

Rosé

I love a darker-hued style, but pale Provence rosé is always a versatile pick. For a similar look at better value, try wines from the Languedoc.

Light to medium-bodied red wine

- **Save** – Cinsault from South Africa or Chile, Rioja Crianza, Barbera.
- **Spend** – Loire Cabernet (France), Beaujolais Villages, Frappato.
- **Splurge** – Pinot Noir (Burgundy, Oregon, California, New Zealand), Garnacha from Spain's Gredos, *Cru* Beaujolais.

Water

- Make sure water is available in abundance! Jugs or bottled water – sparkling is my preference.

BRUNCHING, BEAUTIFULLY

Wine at brunch is a joyous moment. It is often the first sip of the day, so you'll want something fresh and crisp – a style that stimulates the palate and appetite without overwhelming it. Think of wines you'd serve at aperitif hour: sparkling wines, crisp unoaked or lightly oaked whites, fruity and mineral rosés. These pair well with both light and indulgent dishes – the mix of breakfast classics and lunch plates, from eggs and pastries to salads and sandwiches, sweet and savoury. And since brunch is daytime drinking, lighter-alcohol styles tend to go down well.

Best all-round brunch wines

- **Traditional-method sparkling wines** – Particularly fresh, approachable styles, such as French Crémant or even a *Pétillant naturel* (aka Pét-Nat – unfiltered, lightly fizzy, usually lower in alcohol). Rosé sparklings are especially versatile with brunch bites, from eggs and pastries to salads and sweets. To splurge, look to Champagne, English sparkling wine or Franciacorta.
- **Rosé (Provence, pale style)** – Delicate fruit and mineral freshness make this food-friendly wine ideal with tomato dishes (tarts, shakshuka), salmon, light berry plates, and soft cheeses, such as mozzarella or burrata.
- **Sauvignon Blanc** – Crisp, mineral-driven examples from the Loire, New Zealand or Chile pair beautifully with egg-based dishes, tangy cheeses (goats', feta), salads and greens.

The brunch spread

- **Fresh pastries** – Croissants, pain au chocolat, cinnamon buns, mini Danish
- **Quality bread** – Sourdough, ciabatta or bagels served with butter, cream cheese, conserves, honey
- **Seasonal fruit platter** – Berries, stone fruit, tropical fruit
- **Cured and smoked fish** – Smoked salmon, trout gravlax, mackerel
- **Soft cheeses and charcuterie** – Burrata, whipped ricotta, bresaola, mortadella
- **Eggs** – Boiled, baked, frittata, omelettes
- **Leafy salad or avocado with fresh herbs**
- **Heritage tomatoes with lemon vinaigrette**
- **Pancakes or waffles**

Brunchtime serving tips

- Chill all wines well; better a touch too cold than too warm at brunch.
- Keep glassware casual: while most sparkling wines are best in stems, I love a simple tumbler for playful Pét-Nats and still wines at a relaxed brunch.
- Serve dishes on large platters for easy self-serve grazing.

DELICIOUS BRUNCH PAIRINGS

If you're keeping brunch simple rather than a full spread, here are some classic dishes with wines that work brilliantly:

- Avocado on toast with feta – Sauvignon Blanc
- Eggs Benedict – Champagne or similar sparkling wine
- Waffles with bacon and maple syrup – Chenin Blanc rich-style
- Smoked salmon and scrambled eggs – Rosé Champagne or similar sparkling rosé
- Full English breakfast – Beaujolais or similar light red

Brunch recipes in this book

- Sauvignon Blanc with pea and asparagus frittata (see page 154)
- Rosé with beetroot-and-gin-cured salmon (see page 85)
- Pinot Grigio with grilled peach, pine nut and ricotta salad (see page 158)
- Rosé with burrata, strawberries and tomatoes (see page 166)
- Frappato with tomato tart (see page 162)

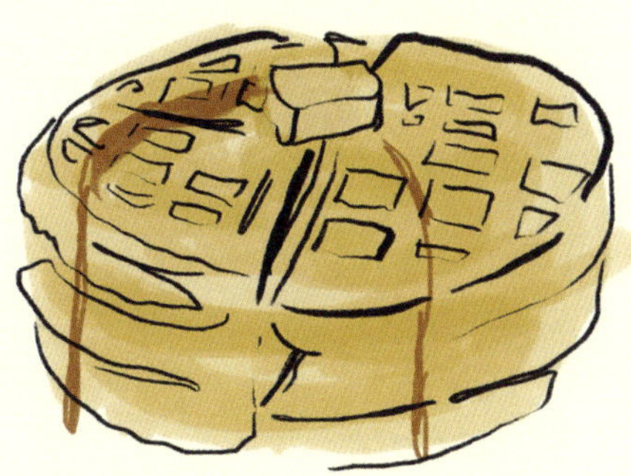

LA DOLCE VITA

For a taste of Italy, here are two themed evenings that showcase some of the country's most wonderful wines: a more casual graze-and-sip evening, followed by a gastronomic evening of indulgent plates and pours. Italy is home to more indigenous grape varieties than anywhere else in the world, and that's what makes it such a special place for wine lovers: there are so many unique grapes and regional identities, stretching from the alpine north to the volcanic soils of Sicily.

APÉRO NIGHT – CASUAL SNACKS AND FRESH WINES

We're recreating that gorgeous Italian apéro-hour vibe at home – that golden moment after work when bars are buzzing, snacks are plentiful, and everyone's in the mood for something fresh and quaffable before the evening unfolds. Lay everything out informally on wooden boards with a bucket of juicy wines on ice for guests to help themselves.

The menu

A spread of bruschetta with different toppings (tomato and basil, prosciutto and fig, aubergine caponata), some olives and crudités, grilled artichokes, Parmesan shavings, focaccia and quality olive oil – easy, unfussy snacks to graze on while standing and chatting.

The wine list

- ✦ **Col Fondo Prosecco** – a more 'natural' style of Prosecco: cloudy, lightly sparkling and dry.
- ✦ **Lambrusco** – a juicy, gently sparkling red with a touch of sweetness and refreshing acidity.
- ✦ **Gavi** – fresh, crisp and zesty, a clean-cut apéro white.
- ✦ **Soave** – elegant and a little more textured than Gavi, with riper fruit and nutty nuances.
- ✦ **Frappato** – a silky, vibrant Sicilian red that's perfect served lightly chilled.

ITALIAN FEAST – CLASSIC AND CLASSY WINES WITH DISHES TO MATCH

Apéro

Start with Franciacorta, the traditional-method sparkling wine from Lombardy. With its rich citrus and brioche flavours and bright acidity, it pairs beautifully with simple, fatty snacks, such as Parmesan crisps, mortadella or mini arancini.

Starter

Next, an Etna Bianco – a citrusy, mineral-driven white grown on the slopes of Mount Etna, usually based on the Carricante grape, ranging from crisp to more textured. Pair the fresher expressions with clams in white wine (see page 93), and the more rounded versions with grilled peach, pine nut and ricotta salad (see page 158).

Main

Consider a tasting of two or three of Italy's signature red grapes: Nebbiolo (perfumed and earthy), Sangiovese (expressive and savoury) and Aglianico (intense and muscular). These wines have high acidity and firm tannins, so they're best served with something rich and robust, such as duck ragu and pappardelle (see page 135). Let's look at the key regions for these grapes.

- ✦ **Piedmont** (Nebbiolo) – From the north, look to Barolo or Barbaresco for benchmark expressions – high quality, but they come with a price tag. Wines labelled Langhe Nebbiolo are typically more approachable and affordable.
- ✦ **Tuscany** (Sangiovese) – From central Italy, Chianti Classico (a smaller, historic subzone) generally delivers higher quality than simple Chianti. I love the 100 per cent Sangiovese wines from Montalcino: Rosso di Montalcino is more accessible (though still serious), while Brunello di Montalcino offers more structure, depth and ageability.
- ✦ **Campania and Basilicata** (Aglianico) – This southern gem offers incredible depth for the price. Some of the best examples come from the Taurasi region.

Dessert

And after a big meal? Let's return to something sparkling – a chilled glass of Moscato d'Asti. Light and fresh, low in alcohol, gently sweet, just a little fizzy – it's a fun and delicious finish after the rich main course. Serve with fruity desserts, white chocolate, dry biscuits, or my white chocolate rainbow bark (see page 179).

VIN ET VOILÀ

Here are two French-themed tastings designed to show two sides of the French wine scene: the timeless classics that set the global benchmark, and the new, low-intervention styles pushing boundaries. France is the reference point for so many grapes and styles around the world, making it the perfect place to revisit, compare and dig into the nuances of different styles.

LOW-INTERVENTION HOTSPOTS

This tasting highlights some of the key French regions associated with 'low-intervention' winemaking. I tend to use this phrase because the word 'natural' can be divisive – it's not always known that some of the world's most prestigious and expensive wines, especially in Burgundy, are made in exactly this way: no chemicals, native yeasts, minimal adjustments, and little interference from machines or vessels. Some of these wines can be spotted via a new certification on the label, the logo *Vin Méthode Nature*, but it's still relatively new. If you're starting to explore these wines, I'd suggest going in person to an independent wine shop or contacting a specialist retailer for tailored advice. This line-up moves naturally from fizz to a light then richer white, and from a light to richer red.

Nibbles

Spiced chickpeas, saucisson and grilled artichokes (see page 82) sit well alongside all these wines, and you could follow through with fried gnocchi, sage and butternut (see page 161) for something more substantial.

The wines

- **Sparkling wine** – Chenin Blanc Pét-Nat, or Crémant from the Loire.
- **White fresh style** – Muscadet Sèvre et Maine, a classic coastal region in the Loire Valley with a low-intervention movement.
- **White richer style** – Savagnin from Jura, oxidative or topped-up ouillé style.
- **Red light style** – Beaujolais, such as Beaujolais Villages, or trade up to a *Cru* such as Morgon or Fleurie.
- **Red richer style** – Languedoc-Roussillon, such as Corbières, Minervois or Fitou (typically blends of Carignan, Grenache, Syrah and Mourvèdre).

CLASSIC FRANCE

This tasting is ideal for six or more people. Begin with a chilled glass of Champagne to spark the appetite, then move into two flights: three whites side by side, followed by three reds. Keep the pours small, giving guests time to taste, take notes and compare what they enjoy about each grape and style. Cheese and charcuterie are perfect to nibble on here. Keep the tasting structured for about 45 minutes, then relax things and bring a simple, versatile dish to the table and let everyone help themselves, topping up their glasses as they like. Mediterranean chicken (see page 123) or chicken, tarragon and pears (see page 128) work brilliantly with both white and red wines. To finish, serve canelés – the traditional Bordeaux pastry, originally made from leftover yolks when the whites were used in winemaking – alongside a glass of Sauternes.

Sparkling wine

- **Champagne** – a classic, elegant sparkling to kick off the night.

Whites

- **Chardonnay** (Burgundy) – pick either unoaked Chablis or a richer Côte de Beaune style (with villages such as Meursault or Puligny-Montrachet if budget allows). If you fancy highlighting the contrast, pour both styles side by side.
- **Sauvignon Blanc** (Loire) – Sancerre or Pouilly-Fumé for benchmark styles.
- **Chenin Blanc** (Loire) – Vouvray or Saumur; pick a dry style for comparison.

Reds

- **Bordeaux Blend** – Left Bank (Cabernet Sauvignon-dominant) or Right Bank (Merlot-dominant), or both if budget permits.
- **Pinot Noir** (Burgundy) – Côte de Nuits (consider the classic villages of Gevrey-Chambertin or Chambolle-Musigny if budget allows).
- **Syrah** (Northern Rhône) – Crozes-Hermitage can be better value; Cornas, Hermitage or Côte-Rôtie for a splurge.

Sweet

- **Sauternes** – Unctuous, honeyed wine made from noble rot-affected grapes, usually a blend of Sauvignon Blanc, Semillon and a small part of Muscadelle.

FIESTA EN CASA

Tapas night has to be one of my favourite themes – especially with a big group, as you can open lots of wines and let the evening unfold with easy, shareable food. Outside the UK, I've spent more time in Spain than anywhere else, and Spanish wines fill me with joy – from refined to rustic, traditional to contemporary, there are so many options to shape a tasting or a whole evening.

This menu highlights some of my favourite bottles that show Spain's diversity, heritage and, above all, its food-friendliness. It works best for six or more guests, and most dishes can be prepped in advance or need little cooking, so you can enjoy time at the table.

Aperitif

Begin with a glass of Cava or Corpinnat. For the very top tier, look for Cava de Paraje Calificado on the label – single-estate wines with long ageing and strict production rules. A step below sits Cava de Guarda Superior (Reserva and Gran Reserva), still a cut above entry-level bottles. Corpinnat is a newer category: artisanal sparkling wines from select producers who broke away from the Cava DO, focusing on organic methods, indigenous grapes and high-quality production. Serve with nibbles, such as jamón ibérico, anchovies and olives (see page 81).

Tapas Round 1

Next, Spain's signature white: Albariño. This Galician gem is now exported worldwide, known for citrus brightness and a saline edge. Entry-level versions are crisp and simple, but spend a little more for texture and complexity. With its high acidity, it's a natural with fried, fishy and fresh dishes, so pair it with:

- Pan con tomate (toasted bread with grated tomato, garlic, olive oil and salt)
- Hot garlicky prawns (shrimp)
- Salt cod fritters
- A simple green salad with good olive oil and sherry vinegar

Cheese course

For a pause between rounds, serve dry Amontillado Sherry – nutty, woody, with a tangy lift – to mirror the cheese's savoury bite. Manchego is the obvious choice – I'd go for a semi-curado (aged 3–6 months) or curado (6–12 months) for extra depth. Add membrillo (quince paste) on the side for a sweet counterpoint.

Tapas Round 2

Now for the reds. Two icons side by side make a great talking point: classic Rioja Reserva and a Mencía from Bierzo. Rioja, one of the world's most-recognized red wines, gains complexity from oak and bottle ageing, often with vanilla and clove notes alongside plush fruit and earthy tones. Mencía, sometimes called Spain's answer to Cabernet Franc, is usually fresher and fruit-driven, with a floral and herbal lift and without overt oak. Comparing these reds is an interesting exercise in looking at two quality regions with quite distinct winemaking styles. Serve the reds with:

- Chorizo cooked in red wine
- Padrón peppers, pan-fried until blistered, then salted
- Patatas bravas (crisp potatoes with spicy sauce)

Sweet finish

To end, I like to keep things low in effort but high in impact: a scoop of vanilla ice cream with a generous drizzle of Pedro Ximénez Sherry, plus a little glass alongside. Pedro Ximénez is dark, sticky and indulgent – all figs, molasses and coffee – and it transforms the simplest ice cream into something wow. I often serve it in little tubs or bowls so everyone can tuck in straight away – delicious.

EXPLORING ISLAND WINES

Take your guests on a little island-hopping journey across these diverse lands that are home to ultra-expressive wines. Here is a suggestion of wines, starting with two whites, followed by two reds and finishing with a sweet fortified wine.

- **Assyrtiko** – Begin on the iconic Greek island of Santorini where Assyrtiko thrives in volcanic soils. When I visited, I was fascinated by the vines trained into little basket-like structures low to the ground, protecting them from the fierce winds and shading the grapes from the sun. Styles range from fresh and citrusy to more textured and complex – but always with bright acidity and a mineral edge, making it the perfect white to start your tasting.

- **Listán Blanco** and **Listán Negro** – Now let's head to Tenerife, the largest of the Canary Islands, where these two grapes produce intense, fresh wines from the island's distinctive black volcanic soils. Listán Blanco (the local name for Palomino) gives crisp, citrus-driven whites with a smoky mineral edge, while Listán Negro makes relatively light reds with vibrant fruit and that signature volcanic streak. Many producers here work in a low-intervention style, and the wines are full of personality.

- **Cannonau** – Then on to Sardinia, an almost tropical-feeling island with white sand beaches and azure seas. Cannonau, the local name for Grenache, produces big-hearted, hedonistic reds packed with ripe, almost jammy red fruit, a touch of herbal nuance and a soft, velvety texture.

- **Malmsey** or **Bual** – Finally, finish with something sweet from the lush island of Madeira. Malmsey is the richest style, Bual a touch less sweet, but both deliver layers of caramel, coffee and fig wrapped in Madeira's trademark electric acidity. A truly indulgent close to your tasting.

A GREEK ODYSSEY

Here we have a journey through Greece, from the mainland to the islands, discovering indigenous varieties and unique wines with Greek-inspired pairing suggestions.

Aperitif

Let's begin with Moschofilero. Grown predominantly in the Peloponnese, it has a pink-tinged skin and produces floral, perfumed white wines with a touch of spice and refreshing acidity – something a little different to start on. Staying with the Greek theme, it's lovely with nibbles such as grilled halloumi with pomegranate seeds, stuffed vine leaves, tzatziki with pitta, and olives.

Starter

In contrast to Moschofilero's aromatic character, Assyrtiko is more mineral-driven, precise and citrusy, making a distinctive follow-on. Indigenous to Santorini, it is also widely planted on other islands and the mainland. Santorini wines command higher prices, but there are excellent, fresh and lively examples from Crete and Macedonia. Assyrtiko is a natural partner to seafood – try it with a sharing platter of prawn saganaki (see page 105).

Main

With a meaty main, pour Greece's flagship red grape, Xinomavro. The finest expressions come from Naoussa and can age gracefully for a decade or more, balancing fruit, perfume and savoury, earthy depth. They are superb with dishes such as harissa lamb cutlets and pistachio (see page 148).

Dessert

Finish with the indulgent Vinsanto from Santorini (not to be confused with Italian Vin Santo). Although sometimes tricky to source, it's worth seeking out in specialist Greek shops. Made from sun-dried grapes, including Assyrtiko, then aged in oak, it offers nutty, dried-fruit and caramel notes – delicious with baklava or tangy blue cheese.

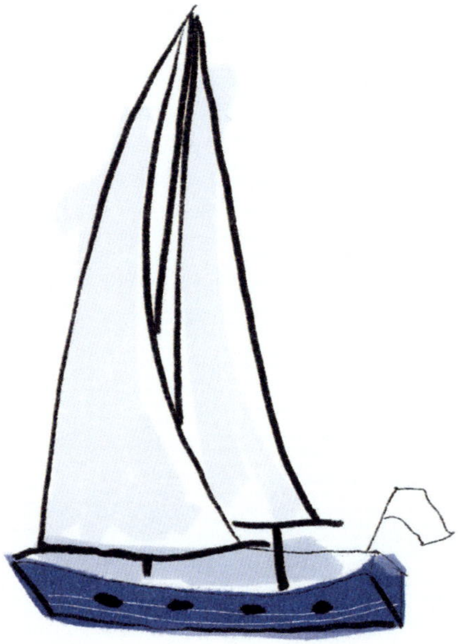

TASTE THE STATES

My journey into wine began while I was living in New York, so wines from the USA hold a special place for me. I visited wineries in California and Long Island, and later discovered the Finger Lakes. Back in the UK, I explored Washington State wines and fell for Oregon after a memorable tasting at the US Embassy in London. There's so much to discover across the States, with new regions gaining recognition and winemakers refining their styles in response to climate and terroir. These tastings focus on wines that are most accessible internationally. We start with a coast-to-coast dinner, then move on to a tour of California from north to south.

FROM COAST TO COAST

A voyage across the states of New York, Oregon and Washington.

Aperitif

- ✦ **Long Island traditional-method sparkling wine** (New York) – The maritime climate here lends itself to grapes that retain lovely crisp freshness. Grape growing focuses on classic Champagne varieties of Chardonnay, Pinot Noir and Pinot Meunier – expect citrus, orchard-fruit and saline notes. Pair with fish goujons, devilled eggs and caviar (see page 73).

Starter

For the starter, compare two white wines with strong reputations for quality:

- ✦ **Finger Lakes Riesling** (New York) – Pick a dry Finger Lakes Riesling grown around the deep glacial lakes – it delivers zesty, floral notes alongside racy acidity – and serve with sea bass crudo (see page 101).
- ✦ **Willamette Valley Chardonnay** (Oregon) – Oregon Chardonnay shows tension and finesse akin to Burgundy styles. Pair with mini crab brioche buns (see page 77).

Main

Next up, a comparison of two or three reds from across the States. These styles pair well with confit duck, blood orange and sweet potato (see page 131).

- ✦ **Willamette Valley Pinot Noir** (Oregon) – Burgundian in spirit, restrained, savoury.
- ✦ **Finger Lakes Cabernet Franc** (New York) – Floral with crunchy red fruit reminiscent of Loire Valley styles.
- ✦ **Washington State Syrah** (look for Walla Walla or Columbia Valley) – Similar to Northern Rhône but typically with more body, ripe black fruit and pepperiness.

A TOUR OF CALIFORNIA

This tasting is ideal for eight or more guests. It flows from the wine regions of northern to southern California, covering many iconic regions and styles, moving from sparkling to white to red. I'd suggest providing guests with a map of California marked with each wine region, road-trip style, so you can follow the route with each glass for context and fun. Begin with your sparkling wine, then serve the two styles of Chardonnay side by side for comparison. Next, divide your reds into a flight of three and then a flight of two.

Sparkling wine

✦ **Anderson Valley traditional-method sparkling** – This northern hotspot in Mendocino is known for its cool climate and high-quality traditional-method sparkling wines; expect ripe citrus, stone fruit and fresh acidity.

Whites

✦ **Sonoma Coast** or **Russian River Chardonnay** – Cooler, coastal spots.

✦ **Napa Valley Chardonnay** – Richer and riper in style.

Red Flight 1

✦ **Zinfandel** – Look for examples from Dry Creek Valley (Sonoma), known for its old-vine plantings delivering bold fruit and spice.

✦ **Cabernet Sauvignon** – From its heartland, Napa Valley: premium-priced, full-bodied, dark fruit and polished, with some producers and sub-regions crafting more restrained Bordeaux-inspired styles.

✦ **Red Rhône blend** (Grenache, Syrah, Mourvèdre) – head to Paso Robles where producers of these Rhône-style wines became known as the 'Rhône Rangers'.

Red Flight 2

✦ **Pinot Noir** – Refined Pinot from the cool Santa Rita Hills, on the western edge of the Santa Ynez Valley: perfumed, savoury and elegant.

✦ **Syrah** – To finish, we move further east within the Santa Ynez Valley for a peppery, elegant expression of Syrah.

As a final note, some of my favourite expressions of Pinot Noir and Syrah come from further north in Sonoma – well worth adding to your discovery list.

HOME WINE ESSENTIALS

Here is a selection of key wine accessories to consider purchasing for home drinking and entertaining, alongside some essential tips on wine storage and serving temperatures for different wines.

Waiter's friend bottle opener
A reliable opener that has a small blade to cut the foil on the bottle and a corkscrew and lever system to pull the cork out of the bottle.

Glassware
I'm a fan of what is known as a universal glass, a one-size-fits-all glass that works for all styles of wine: sparkling, white, red, orange, rosé, sweet, fortified. It usually has a medium-sized bowl and a gentle angled rim inwards which allow for aromas and flavours to be released on a swirl and sip, but to remain concentrated in the glass. For easy hosting, I recommend purchasing more of these glasses rather than having a varied selection of different types.

Sparkling wine stopper
An affordable, handy gadget to keep bubbles intact if you are opening a bottle and not finishing it immediately. Pop the stopper in after pouring, press the lever down and place the sparkling wine back in the fridge to keep bubbles energetic.

Vacuum pump
A simple gadget that works with a pump and vacuum system to extract air from the bottle via a stopper to keep wine fresh for longer. I generally use this for still wines when I haven't finished the bottle. Stored in the fridge after using the vacuum pump, they can keep fresh for 2–5 days, depending on the style.

Ice bucket
An ice bucket is a great accessory for quick chilling of bottles and looks great too. Fill with water and ice and pop your bottle or bottles in for an effective fast chill.

STORAGE

Wines for more immediate drinking (within a month or so) can be kept in the fridge (all styles). For mid-term storage over a few months or longer, a wine fridge is a great investment, keeping wines at a cool, constant temperature and free from artificial light. If a wine fridge isn't an option, then look to keep wines in the coolest spot in your home, away from light and movement from appliances. Keep wines sealed by cork (as opposed to screwcaps) on their sides.

SERVING TEMPERATURES

The experience of enjoying wine can be greatly impacted by the serving temperature. I find the most common issue is serving white wines too cool, which can mute their flavours. They are best served between 7°C (45°F) and 12°C (54°F), depending on the style. Red wines, on the other hand, can be served too warm, which can lead to them feeling flat and lacking energy. They are best served between 12°C (54°F) and 16°C (61°F). Of course, personal preference plays a part in how you enjoy wine, so the following is only rough guidance:

- **Sparkling wines** – Chill in the fridge for 2 hours, serve immediately.
- **Sweet wines** – Chill in the fridge for 2 hours, serve immediately.
- **Light to medium-bodied white wines** – Chill in the fridge for 1½ hours, serve immediately.
- **Full-bodied and oaked white wines** – Chill in the fridge for 1 hour, open 15 minutes before serving.
- **Rosé wines** – Chill in the fridge for 1½ hours, serve immediately.
- **Light to medium-bodied red wines** – Chill in the fridge for 45 minutes, open 15 minutes before serving.
- **Full-bodied red wines** – Chill in the fridge for 30 minutes, open 30 minutes before serving.
- **Orange wines** – Chill in the fridge for 45 minutes, open 15 minutes before serving.
- **Fortified wines** – Treat light-bodied and light-coloured styles (Fino Sherry, for example) like a light to medium-bodied white wine. Treat deeper-coloured, medium to full-bodied styles (vintage Port, for example) like a red wine.

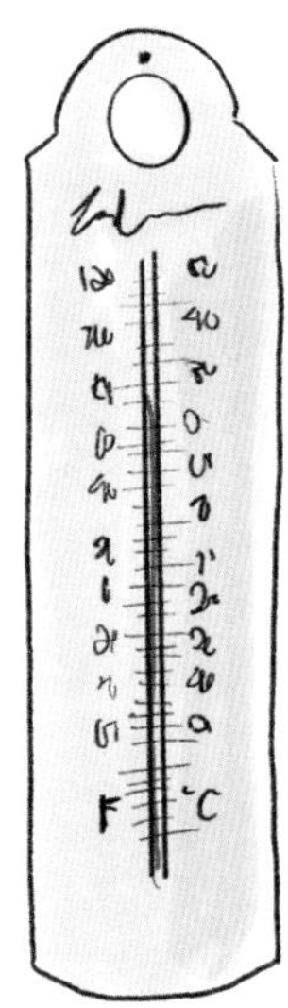

INDEX

INDEX

ACKNOWLEDGEMENTS

This book became a lifeline at a time when I needed one most. My first thank you is to my publisher, Alison Starling – for the opportunity, your calm, guiding presence and for supporting me throughout this project. Thank you for helping me channel a difficult period into something creative and challenging, and for encouraging a book that brings together everything I love: wine, food, hosting, all with a touch of education and lots of style. I am incredibly proud of what we have made.

To my friend for life, creative sidekick, life coach (!) and photographer, Laura – your work in this book is beautiful. I love your spirit and working with you. The shoot days were incredible, and I'm always excited for what's next...

I was so lucky to involve one of my best childhood friends, Elizabeth Pearson, as recipe consultant on this book. Your input was meticulous and invaluable, and the recipe testing was wonderful – full-on, but with plenty of gossiping and laughs, as you can imagine.

It was a pleasure to work with the brilliant team at Octopus again – Juliette and Alex, the dream team – thank you for making this book even more beautiful than the last, and for ensuring the whole process was so collaborative and enjoyable. Thank you to our fabulous illustrator, Kiki; your illustrations once again bring so much soul and character to these pages.

To Natalie Thompson (food stylist) and Max Robinson (prop stylist and hand model extraordinaire) – the shoot days with you both were a joy and a giggle, and of course we created some great art too. Great chats, such a buzz, and I'm in awe of your talent. I'll treasure the memories from those shoot days.

And finally, thank you to my wonderful family, friends and colleagues for their constant support – and for always being up for a glass of Champagne, even when I'm feeling a bit dramatic.

Wine brings people together, and those shared moments stay with us. If we've ever shared a glass, this is my thank you to you.

The shoots for this book were made possible by a number of wonderful partners.

First, thank you, Janina Doyle, for your gargantuan effort coordinating an enormous number of wines and bottles for the shoot days. You are an organization queen, and I couldn't have got there emotionally or physically without your help.

A huge thank you to the many wineries, agencies and PRs who supported the shoots:

Antinori, Arianna Occhipinti, Blandy's, Borgogno, Cave de l'Ormarine, Château de Tracy, Château Guiraud, Cloudy Bay, Domaine Daniel Dugois, Domaine Drouhin Oregon, Domaine Leflaive, Gaia Wines, González Byass, Gramona, Gravner, Grosset, Kopke, Langham Wine Estate, Lustau, Meerlust, Michele Chiarlo, Minuty, Morris of Rutherglen, Nikolaihof, Perrier-Jouët, Ricasoli, Simpsons Wine Estate, Terras Gauda, Tolpuddle Vineyard, William Fèvre.

Bancroft Wines, Berkmann Wine Cellars, Boutinot, Corney & Barrow, Emma Wellings PR, Enotria, EVIVA PR, Fells, González Byass UK, Hallgarten & Novum Wines, Les Caves de Pyrenne, Liberty Wines, Maisons Marques et Domaines, Matthew Clark, Newcomer Wines, Raeburn Fine Wines, The Wine Society.

ABOUT THE AUTHOR

Charlotte Kristensen is a wine columnist, communicator and educator based in London. Prior to focusing on wine, she worked as a lawyer in the City of London. After falling in love with the world of wine while living in New York, Charlotte decided to leave the corporate world and made the leap into wine. In 2018, she set up her Instagram account @thelondonwinegirl to record her journey, and now has followers around the world. Charlotte completed the prestigious Diploma in Wines with the Wine and Spirits Education Trust (WSET) in 2020 and is a certified WSET wine educator. In 2022 she became the weekly wine columnist for *You* magazine at the *Mail on Sunday*. Charlotte runs supper clubs, tastings and events, and works with wine regions and brands from around the world. She is the UK ambassador for Perrier-Jouët.

Charlotte's first book, *Wine Taste Pair Pour*, was published in 2024.

@thelondonwinegirl